THE VOYAGE OF VERRAZZANO:

A CHAPTER IN THE EARLY HISTORY OF MARITIME DISCOVERY IN AMERICA.

BY HENRY C. MURPHY.

NEW YORK
1875.

TO THE

Memory

OF

BUCKINGHAM SMITH,

OF

ST. AUGUSTINE,

FLORIDA.

The following pages, intended to show the claim of discovery in America by Verrazzano to be without any real foundation, belong to a work, in hand, upon the earliest explorations of the coast which have led to the settlement of the United States by Europeans. They are now printed separately, with some additions and necessary changes, in consequence of the recent production of the map of Hieronimo de Verrazano, which professes to represent this discovery, and is therefore supposed to afford some proof of its authenticity; in which view it has been the subject of a learned and elaborate memoir by J. Carson Brevoort Esq.

Certain important documents in relation to Verrazzano, procured from the archives of Spain and Portugal by the late Buckingham Smith, on a visit to those countries a year or two before his death, are appended. They were intended to accompany a second edition of his *Inquiry*, a purpose which has been interrupted by his decease. They were entrusted by him to the care of his friend, George H. Moore Esq., of New York, who has placed them at our disposal on the present occasion.

The fragmentary and distorted form in which the letter ascribed to Verrazzano, appeared in the collection of Ramusio, and was thence universally admitted into history, rendered it necessary that the letter should be here given complete, according to its original meaning. It is, therefore, annexed in the English translation of Dr. Cogswell, which though not entirely unexceptionable is, for all purposes, sufficiently accurate. The original Italian text can, however, be consulted in the Collections of the New York Historical Society, accompanying his translation, and also in the Archivio Storico Italiano, in which it is represented by the editor to be more correctly copied from the manuscript, and amended in its language where it seemed corrupt; but such corrections are few and unimportant. In all cases in which the letter is now made the subject of critical examination, the passages referred to are given, for obvious reasons, according to the reading of the Florentine editor.

We are indebted to the American Geographical Society of New York for the use of its photographs of the Verrazano map, and to Mr. Brevoort for a copy of the cosmography of Alfonse, from which the chart of Norumbega has been taken. And our thanks are due to Dr. J. Gilmary Shea of New York, for valuable assistance; and to Dr. E. R. Straznicky of the Astor Library, Mons. C. Maunoir of the Société de Géographie of Paris, Dr. J. Hammond Trumbull of Hartford, Hon. John R. Bartlett of Providence, and James Lenox Esq. of New York, for various favors kindly rendered during the progress of our researches.

BROOKLYN, *Sept.* 1875.

CONTENTS.

	Page
I. The Discovery Attributed to Verrazzano,	1–9
II. The Verrazzano Letter not Genuine,	10–24
III. The Letter untrue. I. No Voyage or Discovery made for the King of France, as it states,	25–44
IV. II. Misrepresentations in regard to the Geography of the Coast. The Chesapeake. The Island of Louise. Massachusetts Bay,	45–56
V. III. Cape Breton and the Southerly Coast of Newfoundland, here claimed to have been discovered, were known previously. Perversion of the Text of the Letter by Ramusio,	57–69
VI. IV. The Description of the People and Productions of the Land not made from the Personal Observation of the Writer of the Letter. What distinctively belonged to the Natives is unnoticed, and what is originally mentioned of them is untrue. Further important Alterations of the Text by Ramusio,	69–83
VII. The Extrinsic Evidence in Support of the Claim. I. Discourse of the French Sea Captain of Dieppe,	84–90
VIII. II. The Verrazano Map. It is not an Authoritative Exposition of the Verrazzano Discovery. Its Origin and Date in its present Form. The Letter of Annibal Caro. The Map presented to Henry VIII. Voyages of Verrazzano. The Globe of Euphrosynus Ulpius,	91–115

VIII   CONTENTS.

Page

IX. The Letter to the King founded on the Discoveries of Estévan Gomez. The History of Gomez and his Voyage. The Publication of his Discoveries in Spain and Italy before the Verrazzano claim. The Voyage described in the Letter traced to Ribero's Map of the Discoveries of Gomez, . . 116–133

X. The Career of Verrazzano. An Adventurous Life and Ignominious Death. Conclusion, . . 134–151

Appendix, ... 154–186

Index. 187–197

ILLUSTRATIONS.

The Caravel, ... 9
Arms of the Dauphin, afterwards Henry II, . . . 44
Cape Henry and Entrance into the Chesapeake, . . 56
Birch-Bark Canoe, ... 83

MAPS.

Facing page

Chart from the Cosmography of Jean Alfonse, . . . 37
Map of Hieronomo de Verrazano, of the alleged Discovery and adjacent Countries, only, ... 91
Map from the Globe of Ulpius, of the same, . . . 114
Map of Diego Ribero, showing the Exploration of Gomez and the alleged Track of Verrazzano, . . 129
Map of Verrazano entire, at the End of the Volume.

THE

VOYAGE OF VERRAZZANO:

A CHAPTER IN THE EARLY HISTORY OF MARITIME
DISCOVERY IN AMERICA.

I.

THE DISCOVERY ATTRIBUTED TO VERRAZZANO.

The discovery of the greater portion of the Atlantic coast of North America, embracing all of the United States north of Cape Roman in South Carolina, and of the northern British provinces as far at least as Cape Breton, by Giovanni da Verrazzano, a Florentine, in the service of the king of France, has received until quite recently the assent of all the geographers and historians who have taken occasion to treat of the subject. This acknowledgment, for more than three hundred years, which would seem to preclude all question in regard to its authenticity at this late day, has, however, been due more to the peculiar circumstances of its publication than to any evidence of its truth. The only account of it which exists, is contained in a letter purporting to have been written by the discoverer himself, and is not corroborated by the testimony of any other person, or sustained by any documentary proof. It was not published to the world until it appeared for the first time in Italy, the birth place of the navigator, more than thirty years after the transactions to which it relates are alleged to have taken place; and it has not, up to the present time, received any confirmation in the history of France, whose sovereign, it is asserted, sent forth the expedition, and to whose crown the right of the discovery accordingly attached. Yet it is not difficult to comprehend how the story, appealing to the patriotic sympathies of Ramusio, was inconsiderately adopted by him, and inserted in his famous collection of voyages, and thus receiving his sanction, was not unwillingly accepted, upon his authority, by the French nation, whose glory it advanced, without possibly its having any real foundation. And as there never was any colonization or attempt at possession of the country in consequence of the alleged discovery, or any assertion of title under it, except in a single instance of a comparatively modern date, and with no important bearing, it is no less easy to understand, how thus adopted and promulgated by the only countries interested in the question, the claim was admitted by other nations without challenge or dispute, and has thus become incorporated into modern history without investigation.

Although the claim has never been regarded of any practical importance in the settlement of the country, it has nevertheless possessed an historical and geographical interest in connection with the origin and progress of maritime discovery on this continent. Our own writers assuming its validity, without investigation, have been content to trace, if possible, the route of Verrazzano and point out the places he explored, seeking merely to reconcile the account with the actual condition and situation of the country. Their explanations, though sometimes plausible, are often contradictory, and not unfrequently absurd. Led into an examination of its merits with impressions in its favor, we have nevertheless been compelled to adopt the conclusion of a late American writer, that it is utterly fictitious.[1] The grounds upon which our conviction rests we propose now to state. Some documents will be introduced, for the first time here brought to light, which will serve further to elucidate the question, and show the career and ultimate fate of Verrazzano.

The letter, in which the pretension is advanced, professes to be addressed by Verrazzano to the king of France, at that time Francis I, from Dieppe, in Normandy, the 8th of July (O. S.), 1524, on his return to that port from a voyage, undertaken by order of the king, for the purpose of finding new countries; and to give an account of the discoveries which he had accordingly made. He first reminds his majesty that, after starting with four ships, originally composing the expedition, he was compelled by storms, encountered on the northern coasts, to put into Brittany in distress, with the loss of two of them; and that after repairing there the others, called the Normanda and Delfina (*Dauphine*), he made a cruize with this *fleet of war*, as they are styled, along the coast of Spain. He finally proceeded on the voyage of discovery with the Dauphine

---

[1] *An Inquiry into the Authenticity of Documents concerning a Discovery in North America claimed to have been made by Verrazzano. Read before the New York Historical Society, Tuesday, October 4th, 1864. By Buckingham Smith.* New York, 1864. pp. 31, and a map.

alone, setting sail from a desolate rock near the island of Madeira, on the 17th of January, 1524, with fifty men, and provisions for eight months, besides the necessary munitions of war. This voyage, therefore, is to be regarded, according to the representations here made, to have been begun with the sailing of the four ships, from Dieppe, in the preceding year.[1] On leaving Madeira they pursued a westerly course for eight hundred leagues and then, inclining a little to the north, ran four hundred leagues more, when on the 7th of March[2] they fell upon a "country never before seen by any one either in ancient or modern times." It seemed very low and stretched to the south, in which direction they sailed along it for the purpose of finding a harbor wherein their ship might ride in safety; but *discovering none* in a distance of fifty

---

[1] Some writers have regarded this introductory as referring to two voyages or cruizes, one with the four ships before the disaster, and the other with the Dauphine afterwards. But it seems clear from their being described as assailed by tempests in the north, which compelled them to run into Brittany for safety, that they were not far distant from Dieppe when the storms overtook them; and must have been either on their way out or on their return to that port. If they were on their return from a voyage to America, as Charlevoix infers (*Fastes Chronologiques*, 1523-4), or simply from a cruize, as Mr. Brevoort supposes, they would, after making their repairs, have proceeded home to Dieppe, instead of making a second voyage. They must, therefore, be regarded as on their way from Dieppe. The idea of a voyage having been performed before the storms, seems to be due to an alteration which Ramusio made in this portion of the letter, by introducing the word "success," as of the four ships. Charlevoix expressly refers to Ramusio as his authority and Mr. Brevoort, makes a paraphrase from the Carli and Ramusio versions combined. (*Notes on the Verrazano Map* in *Journal of the Am. Geog. Society of New York*, vol. IV, pp. 172-3.)

[2] There is some ambiguity in the account, as to the time when they first saw land. The letter reads as follows: "On the 17th of last January we set sail from a desolate rock near the island of Madeira, and sailing westward, in twenty-five days we ran eight hundred leagues. On the 24th of February, we encountered as violent a hurricane as any ship ever weathered. Pursuing our voyage toward the west, a little northwardly, in twenty-four days more, having run four hundred leagues, we reached a new

THE VOYAGE.   5

leagues, they retraced their course, and ran to the north with no better success. They therefore drew in with the land and sent a boat ashore, and had their first communication with the inhabitants, who regarded them with wonder. These people are described as going naked, except around their loins, and as being *black*. The land, rising somewhat from the shore, was covered with thick forests, which sent forth the sweetest fragrance to a great distance. They supposed it adjoined the Orient, and for that reason was not devoid of medicinal and aromatic drugs and gold; and being *in latitude* 34° N., was possessed of a pure, salubrious and healthy climate. They sailed thence westerly for a short distance and then northerly, when at the end of fifty leagues they arrived before a land of great forests, where they landed and found luxuriant vines entwining the trees and producing *sweet and luscious grapes of which they ate*, tasting not unlike their own; and from whence they carried off a boy about eight years old, for the purpose of taking him to France. Coasting thence northeasterly for one hundred leagues, *sailing only in the day time and not making any harbor* in the whole of that distance, they came to a pleasant situation among steep hills, from whence a large river ran into the sea. Leaving, in consequence of a rising

---

country," &c. If the twenty-four days be calculated from the 24th of February, the landfall would have taken place on the 20th of March ; but if reckoned from the first twenty-five days run, it would have been on the 7th of that month. Ramusio changes the distance first sailed from 800 to 500 leagues ; the day when they encountered the storm from the 24th to the 20th of February ; and the twenty-four days last run to twenty-five ; making the landfall occur on the 17th or 10th of March according to the mode of calculating the days last run. As it is stated, afterwards, that they encountered a gale *while at anchor on the coast, early* in March, the 7th of that month must be taken as the time of the landfall.

storm, this river, into which they had entered for a short distance with their boat, and where they saw many of the natives in their *canoes*, they sailed directly *east* for eighty leagues, when they discovered an island of triangular shape, about ten leagues from the main land, *equal in size to the island of Rhodes.* This island they named after the mother of the king of France. *Without landing upon it*, they proceeded to a harbor fifteen leagues beyond, at the entrance of a large bay, *twelve leagues broad*, where they came to anchor and remained for fifteen days. They encountered here a people with whom they formed a great friendship, different in appearance from the natives whom they first saw, — these having a *white complexion.* The men were tall and well formed, and the women graceful and possessed of pleasing manners. There were two kings among them, who were attended in state by their gentlemen, and a queen who had her waiting maids. This country was situated in latitude 41° 40′ N, in the parallel of Rome; and was very fertile and abounded with game. They left it on the 6th of May, and sailed one hundred and fifty leagues, *constantly in sight of the land* which stretched to the east. In this long distance *they made no landing*, but proceeded fifty leagues further along the land, which inclined more to the north, when they went ashore and found a people exceedingly barbarous and hostile. Leaving them and continuing their course northeasterly for fifty leagues *further*, they discovered within that distance thirty-two islands. And finally, after having sailed between east and north one hundred and fifty leagues *more*, they reached the fiftieth degree of north latitude, where the Portuguese had commenced their discoveries towards the Arctic circle; when finding their provisions nearly exhausted, they took in wood and water and returned to France, having coasted, it is stated, along an *unknown country for seven hundred leagues.* In conclusion, it is added, they had found it inhabited by a people without religion, but easily to be persuaded, and imitating with fervor the acts of Christian worship performed by the discoverers.

The description of the voyage is followed by what the writer calls a cosmography, in which is shown the distance they had sailed from the time they left the desert rocks at Madeira, and the probable size of the new world as compared with the old, with the relative area of land and water on the whole globe. There is nothing striking or important in this supplement, except that it emphasizes and enforces the statements of the former part of the letter in regard to the landfall, fixes the exact point of their departure from the coast for home again at 50° N. latitude, and gives seven hundred leagues as the extent of the discovery. The length of a longitudinal degree along the parallel of thirty-four, in which it is reiterated they first made land, and between which and the parallel of thirty-two they had sailed from the Desertas, is calculated and found to be fifty-two miles, and the whole number of degrees which they had traversed across the ocean between those parallels, being twelve hundred leagues, or forty-eight hundred miles, is by simple division made ninety-two. The object of this calculation is not apparent, and strikes the reader as if it were a feeble imitation of the manner in which Amerigo Vespucci illustrates his letters. A statement is made, that they took the sun's altitude from day to day, and noted the observations, together with the rise and fall of the tide, in a little book, which was " communicated to his majesty, in the hope of promoting science." It is also mentioned that they had no lunar eclipses, by means of which they could have ascertained the longitude during the voyage. This fact is shown by the tables of Regiomontanus, which had been published long before the alleged voyage, and were open to the world. The statement of it here, therefore, does not, as has been supposed, furnish any evidence in support of the narrative, by reason of its originality.

Such is the account, in brief, which the letter gives of the origin, nature and extent of the alleged discovery; and as it assumes to be the production of the navigator himself, and is the only source of information on the subject, it suggests all the questions which arise in this inquiry. These relate both to the genuineness of the letter, and the truth of its statements; and accordingly bring under consideration the circumstances under which that instrument was made known and has received credit; the alleged promotion of the voyage by the king of France; and the results claimed to have been accomplished thereby. It will be made to appear upon this examination, that the letter, according to the evidence upon which its existence is predicated, could not have been written by Verrazzano; that the instrumentality of the king of France, in any such expedition of discovery as therein described, is unsupported by the history of that country, and is inconsistent with the acknowledged acts of Francis and his successors, and therefore incredible;

and that its description of the coast and some of the physical characteristics of the people and of the country are essentially false, and prove that the writer could not have made them from his own personal knowledge and experience, as pretended. And, in conclusion, it will be shown that its apparent knowledge of the direction and extent of the coast was derived from the exploration of Estevan Gomez, a Portuguese pilot in the service of the king of Spain, and that Verrazzano, at the time of his pretended discovery, was actually engaged in a corsairial expedition, sailing under the French flag, in a different part of the ocean.

THE CARAVEL.

II.

The Verrazzano Letter not Genuine.

No proof that the letter ascribed to Verrazzano, was written by him, has ever been produced. The letter itself has never been exhibited, or referred to in any authentic document, or mentioned by any contemporary or later historian as being in existence, and although it falls within the era of modern history, not a single fact which it professes to describe relating to the fitting out of the expedition, the voyage, or the discovery, is corroborated by other testimony, whereby its genuineness might even be inferred. The only evidence in regard to it, relates to two copies, as they purport to be, both in the Italian language, one of them coming to us printed and the other in manuscript, but neither of them traceable to the alleged original. They are both of them of uncertain date. The printed copy appears in the work of Ramusio, first published in 1556, when Verrazzano and Francis I, the parties to it, were both dead, and a generation of men had almost passed away since the events which it announced had, according to its authority, taken place, and probably no one connected with the government of France at that time could have survived to gainsay the story, were it untrue.[1] Ramusio does not state when or how he

---

[1] Verrazzano died in 1527; Louise, the mother of Francis I in September, 1532; and Francis himself in March, 1547.

obtained what he published. In the preface to the volume in which it is printed, dated three years before, he merely speaks of the narrative incidentally, but in a discourse preceding it, he obscurely alludes to the place where he found it, remarking that it was the only letter of Verrazzano that he had " been able to have, because the others had got astray in the troubles of the unfortunate city of Florence." The origin of the manuscript version is equally involved in mystery. It forms part of a codex which contains also a copy of a letter purporting to have been written by Fernando Carli, from Lyons to his father in Florence, on the 4th of August, 1524, giving an account of the arrival of Verrazzano at Dieppe, and inclosing a copy of his letter to the King. The epistles of Carli and Verrazzano are thus connected together in the manuscript in fact, and by reference in that of Carli, making the copy of the Verrazzano letter a part of Carli's, and so to relate to the same date. But as the Carli letter in the manuscript is itself only a copy, there is nothing to show when that was really written; nor is it stated when the manuscript itself was made. All that is positively known in regard to the latter is, that it was mentioned in 1768, as being then in existence in the Strozzi library in Florence. When it came into that collection does not appear, but as that library was not founded until 1627, its history cannot be traced before that year.[1] Its chirography, however, in the opinion of some competent persons who have examined it, indicates that it was written in the middle of the sixteenth century.

---

[1] *Iter Italicum von D. Friedrich Blume.* Band II, 81. Halle, 1827.

12   VERRAZZANO.

There is, therefore, nothing in the history or character of the publication in Ramusio or the manuscript, to show that the letter emanated from Verrazzano. Neither of them is traceable to him; neither of them was printed at a time when its publication, without contradiction, might be regarded as an admission or acknowledgment by the world of a genuine original; and neither of them is found to have existed early enough to authorize an inference in favor of such an original by reason of their giving the earliest account of the coasts and country claimed to have been discovered. On the contrary, these two documents of themselves, when their nature and origin are rightly understood, serve to prove that the Verrazzano letter is not a genuine production. For this purpose it will be necessary to state more fully their history and character.

The existence of the copy which, in consequence of its connection in the same manuscript with that of the Carli letter, may be designated as the Carli version, is first mentioned in an eulogy or life of Verrazzano in the series of portraits of illustrious Tuscans, printed in Florence in 1767 – 8, as existing in the Strozzi library.[1] The author calls attention to the fact, that it contains a part of the letter which is omitted by Ramusio. In another eulogy of the navigator, by a different hand, G. P. (Pelli), put forth by the same printer in the following year, the writer, referring to the publication of the letter of Ramusio, states that an addition to it, describing the distances to the places

---

[1] *Serie di Ritratti d' Uomini Illustri Toscani con gli elogj istorici dei medesimi.* Vol. secondo. Firenze, 1768.

where Verrazzano had been, was inserted in writing in a copy of the work of Ramusio, in the possession at that time of the Verrazzano family in Florence. These references were intended to show the existence of the cosmography, which Tiraboschi afterwards mentions, giving, however, the first named eulogy as his authority. No portion of the Carli copy appeared in print until 1841, when through the instrumentality of Mr. Greene, the American consul at Rome, it was printed in the collections of the New York Historical Society, accompanied by a translation into English by the late Dr. Cogswell. It was subsequently printed in the Archivio Storico Italiano at Florence, in 1853, with some immaterial corrections, and a preliminary discourse on Verrazzano, by M. Arcangeli. From an inspection of the codex in the library, where it then existed in Florence, M. Arcangeli supposes the manuscript was written in the middle of the sixteenth century. This identical copy was, therefore, probably in existence when Ramusio published his work. Upon comparing the letter as given by Ramusio with the manuscript, the former, besides wanting the cosmography, is found to differ from the latter almost entirely in language, and very materially in substance, though agreeing with it in its elementary character and purpose. The two, therefore, cannot be copies of the same original. Either they are different versions from some other language, or one of them must be a recomposition of the other in the language in which they now are found. In regard to their being both translated from the French, the only other language in which the letter can be supposed to have been written besides the native tongue of Verrazzano, although it is indeed most reasonable to suppose that such a letter, addressed to the king of France, on the results of an expedition of the crown, by an officer in his service, would have been written in that language, it is, nevertheless, highly improbable that any letter could, in this instance, have been so addressed to the King, and two different translations made from it into Italian, one by Carli in Lyons in 1524, and the other by Ramusio in Venice twenty-nine years afterwards, and yet no copy of it in French, or any memorial of its existence in that language be known. This explanation must therefore be abandoned. If on the other hand, one of these copies was so rendered from the French, or from an original in either form in which it appears in Italian, whether by Verrazzano or not, the other must have been rewritten from it. It is evident, however, that the Carli version could not have been derived from that contained in Ramusio, because it contains an entire part consisting of several pages, embracing the cosmographical explanations of the voyage, not found in the latter. As we are restricted to these two copies as the sole authority for the letter, and are, therefore, governed in any conclusion on this subject by what they teach, it must be determined that the letter in Ramusio is a version of that contained in the Carli manuscript. This suggestion is not new. It was made by Mr. Greene in his monograph on Verrazzano, without his following it to the conclusion to which it inevitably leads. If the version in Ramusio be a recomposition of the Carli copy, an important step is gained towards determining the origin of the Verrazzano letter, as in that case the inquiry is brought down to the consideration of the authenticity of the Carli letter, of which it forms a part. But before proceeding to that question, the reasons assigned by Mr. Greene, and some incidental facts stated by him in connection with them, should be given. He says:

"The Strozzi Library is no longer in existence; but the manuscripts of that collection passed into the hands of the Tuscan government, and were divided between the Magliabechian and Laurentian libraries of Florence. The historical documents were deposited in the former. Among them was the cosmographical narration of Verrazzano mentioned by Tiraboschi, and which Mr. Bancroft expresses a desire to see copied for the Historical Society of New York. It is contained in a volume of Miscellanies, marked "Class XIII. Cod. 89. Verraz;" and forms the concluding portion of the letter to Francis the First, which is copied at length in the same volume. It is written in the common running hand of the sixteenth century (*carrattere corsivo*), tolerably distinct, but badly pointed. The whole volume, which is composed of miscellaneous pieces, chiefly relating to contemporary history, is evidently the *work of the same hand*.

"Upon collating this manuscript with that part of the letter which was published by Ramusio, we were struck with the differences in language which run through every paragraph of the two texts. In substance there is no important difference,[1] except in one instance, where, by an evident blunder of the transcriber, *bianchissimo* is put for *branzino*. There is something so peculiar in the style of this letter, as it reads in the manuscript of the Magliabechian, that it is impossible to account for its variations from Ramusio, except by supposing that this editor worked the whole piece over anew, correcting the errors of language upon his own authority.[2] These

---

[1] In this statement Mr. Greene was mistaken, as will be manifested in a comparison of the two texts hereafter given, in which the difference of language will also appear.

[2] Mr. Greene adds in a note to this passage: " He did so also with the translation of Marco Polo. See Apostolo Zeno, Annot. alla Bib. Ital. del Fontanini, tom. II, p. 300; ed. di Parma. 1804." There is another instance mentioned by Amoretti, in the preface to his translation of Pigafetta's journal of Magellan's voyage, and that was with Fabre's translation of the copy of the journal given by Pigafetta to the mother of Francis I. *Premier voyage autour du monde*. xxxii. (Jansen, Paris l'an IX.)

errors indeed are numerous, and the whole exhibits a strange mixture of Latinisms [1] and absolute barbarisms with pure Tuscan words and phrases. The general cast of it, however, is simple and not unpleasing. The obscurity of many of the sentences is, in a great measure, owing to false pointing.

"The cosmographical description forms the last three pages of the letter. It was doubtless intentionally omitted by Ramusio, though it would be difficult to say why. Some of the readings are apparently corrupt; nor, ignorant as we are of nautical science, was it in our power to correct them. There are also some slight mistakes, which must be attributed to the transcriber.

"A letter which follows that of Verrazzano, gives, as it seems to us, a sufficient explanation of the origin of this manuscript. It was written by a young Florentine, named Fernando Carli, and is addressed from Lyons to his father in Florence. It mentions the arrival of Verrazzano at Dieppe, and contains several circumstances about him, which throw a new though still a feeble light upon parts of his history, hitherto wholly unknown. It is by the discovery of this letter, that we have been enabled to form a sketch of him, somewhat more complete than any which has ever yet been given.

"The history of both manuscripts is probably as follows: Carli wrote to his father, thinking, as he himself tells it, that the news of Verrazzano's return would give great satisfaction to many of their friends in Florence. He added at the same time, and this also we learn from his own words, a copy of Verrazzano's letter to the king. Both his letter and his copy of Verrazzano's were intended to be shown to his Florentine acquaintances. Copies, as is usual in such cases, were taken of them; and to us it seems evident that from some one of these the copy in the Magliabechian manuscript was derived. The appearance of this last, which was prepared for some individual fond of collecting miscellaneous documents, if not by him, is a sufficient corroboration of our statement." [2]

Adopting the Carli copy as the primitive form of the Verrazzano letter, and the Carli letter as the original means by which it has been communicated to

---

[1] An instance of these Latinisms is the signature "Janus Verrazzanus," affixed to the letter.

[2] *Historical Studies:* by George Washington Greene, New York, 1850; p. 323. *Life and Voyages of Verrazzano* (by the same), in the *North American Review* for October, 1837. (Vol. 45, p. 306).

the world, the inquiry is resolved into the authenticity of the Carli letter. There are sufficient reasons to denounce this letter as a pure invention; and in order to present those reasons more clearly, we here give a translation of it in full:

Letter of Fernando Carli to his Father. [1]

In the name of God.

4 August, 1524.

Honorable Father:

Considering that when I was in the armada in Barbary at Garbich the news were advised you daily from the illustrious Sig. Don Hugo de Moncada, Captain General of the Cæsarean Majesty in those barbarous parts, [of what] happened in contending with the Moors of that island; by which it appears you caused pleasure to many of our patrons and friends and congratulated yourselves on the victory achieved: so there being here news recently of the arrival of Captain Giovanni da Verrazzano, our Florentine, at the port of Dieppe, in Normandy, with his ship, the Dauphiny, with which he sailed from the Canary islands the end of last January, to go in search of new lands for this most serene crown of France, in which he displayed very noble and great courage in undertaking such an unknown voyage with only one ship, which was a caravel of hardly — tons, with only fifty men, with the intention, if possible, of discovering Cathay, taking a course through other climates than those the Portuguese use in reaching it by the way of Calicut, but going towards the northwest and north, entirely believing that, although Ptolemy, Aristotle and other cosmographers affirm that no land is to be found towards such climates, he would find it there nevertheless. And so God has vouchsafed him as he distinctly describes in a letter of his to this S. M.; *of which, in this, there is a copy.* And for want of provisions, after many months spent in navigating, he asserts he was forced to return from that hemisphere into this, and having been

---

[1] The letter of Carli was first published in 1844, with the discourse of Mr. Greene on Verrazzano, in the *Saggiatore* (I, 257), a Roman journal of history, the fine arts and philology. (M. Arcangeli, *Discorso sopra Giovanni da Verrazzano*, p. 35, in *Archivio Storico Italiano*. Appendice tom. IX.) It will be found in our appendix, according to the reprint in the latter work.

seven months on the voyage, to show a very great and rapid passage, and to have achieved a wonderful and most extraordinary feat according to those who understand the seamanship of the world. Of which at the commencement of his said voyage there was an unfavorable opinion formed, and many thought there would be no more news either of him or of his vessel, but that he might be lost on that side of Norway, in consequence of the great ice which is in that northern ocean; but the Great God, as the Moor said, in order to give us every day proofs of his infinite power and show us how admirable is this worldly machine, has disclosed to him a breadth of land, as you will perceive, of such extent that according to good reasons, and the degrees of latitude and longitude, he alleges and shows it greater than Europe, Africa and a part of Asia; *ergo mundus novus*: and this exclusive of what the Spaniards have discovered in several years in the west; as it is hardly a year since Fernando Magellan returned, who discovered a great country with one ship out of the five sent on the discovery. From whence he brought spices much more excellent than the usual; and of his other ships no news has transpired for five years. They are supposed to be lost. What this our captain has brought he does not state in this letter, except a very young man taken from those countries; but it is supposed he has brought a sample of gold which they do not value in those parts, and of drugs and other aromatic liquors for the purpose of conferring here with several merchants after he shall have been in the presence of the Most Serene Majesty. And at this hour he ought to be there, and from choice to come here shortly, as he is much desired in order to converse with him; the more so that he will find here the Majesty, the King, our Lord, who is expected here in three or four days. And we hope that S. M. will entrust him again with half a dozen good vessels and that he will return to the voyage. And if our Francisco Carli be returned from Cairo, advise him to go, at a venture, on the said voyage with him; and I believe they were acquainted at Cairo where he has been several years; and not only in Egypt and Syria, but almost through all the known world, and thence by reason of his merit is esteemed another Amerigo Vespucci, another Fernando Magellan and even more; and we hope that being provided with other good ships and vessels, well built and properly victualled, he may discover some profitable traffic and matter; and will, our Lord God granting him life, do honor to our country, in acquiring immortal fame and memory. And Alderotto Brunelleschi who started with him and by chance turning back was not willing to accompany him further, will, when he hears of this, be discontented. Nothing else now occurs to me, as I have advised you by others of what is necessary. I commend myself constantly to you, praying you to impart this to our friends, not forgetting Pierfrancesco Dagaghiano who in consequence of being an experienced person will take much pleasure in it, and commend me to him. Likewise to Rustichi, who will not be displeased, if he delight, as usual, in learning matters of cosmography. God guard you from all evil. Your son.

FERNANDO CARLI, in Lyons.

This letter bears date only twenty-seven days after that of the Verrazzano letter, which is declared to be inclosed. To discover its fraudulent nature and the imposition it seeks to practise, it is only necessary to bear this fact in mind, with its pretended origin, in connection with the warlike condition of France and the personal movements of the king, immediately preceding and during the interval between the dates of the two letters. It purports to have been written by Fernando Carli to his father in Florence. Carli is not an uncommon Italian name and probably existed in Florence at that time, but who this Fernando was, has never transpired. He gives in this letter all there is of his biography, which is short. He had formerly been in the service of the emperor, Charles V, under Moncada, in the fleet sent against the Moors in Barbary, and was then in Lyons, where, it might be inferred, from a reference to its merchants, that he was engaged in some mercantile pursuit; but the reason of his presence there is really unaccounted for. It is not pretended that he held any official position under the king of France. The name of his father, by means of which his lineage might be traced, is not mentioned, but Francisco Carli is named as of the same family, but without designating his relationship.

Whether a myth or a reality, Fernando seems to have been an obscure person, at the best; not known to the political or literary history of the period, and not professing to occupy any position, by which he might be supposed to have any facility or advantage for obtaining official information or the news of the day, over the other inhabitants of Lyons and of France.

He is made to say that he writes this letter for the particular purpose of communicating to his father and their friends in Florence, the news, which had reached Lyons, of the arrival of Verrazzano from his wonderful and successful voyage of discovery, and that he had advised his parent of all other matters touching his own interests, by another conveyance. It might be supposed and indeed reasonably expected in a letter thus expressly devoted to Verrazzano, that some circumstance, personal or otherwise, connected with the navigator or the voyage, or some incident of his discovery, besides what was contained in the enclosed letter, such as must have reached Lyons, with the news of the return of the expedition, would have been mentioned, especially, as it would all have been interesting to Florentines. But nothing of the kind is related. Nothing appears in the letter in regard to the expedition that is not found in the Verrazzano letter.[1] What is stated in reference to the previous life of Verrazzano, must have been as well known to Carli's father as to himself, if it were true, and is therefore

---

[1] Mr. Greene, in his life of Verrazzano, remarks that it appears from Carli's letter, that the Indian boy whom Verrazzano is stated to have carried away, arrived safely in France; but that is not so. What is said in that letter is, that Verrazzano does not mention *in his letter* what he had brought home, except this boy.

unnecessarily introduced, and the same may be said of the facts stated in regard to Brunelleschi's starting on the voyage with Verrazzano and afterwards turning back. The particular description of Dagaghiano and Rustichi, both of Florence, the one as a man of experience and the other as a sudent of cosmography, was equally superfluous in speaking of them to his father. These portions of the letter look like flimsy artifices to give the main story the appearance of truth. They may or may not have been true, and it is not inconsistent with an intention to deceive in regard to the voyage that they should have been either the one or the other. A single allusion, however, is made to the critical condition of affairs in France and the stirring scenes which were being enacted on either side of the city of Lyons at the moment the letter bears date. It is the mention of the expected arrival of the king at Lyons within three or four days. It is not stated for what purpose he was coming, but the fact was that Francis had taken the field in person to repel the Spanish invasion in the south of France, and was then on his way to that portion of his kingdom, by way of Lyons, where he arrived a few days afterwards. The reference to this march of the king fixes beyond all question the date of the letter, as really intended for the 4th of August, 1524.

The movements of Francis at this crisis become important in view of the possibility of the publication in any form of the Verrazzano letter at Lyons, at the last mentioned date, or of the possession of a copy of it there as claimed by Carli in his letter. The army of the emperor, under Pescara and Bourbon, crossed the

Alps and entered Provence early in July, and before the date of the Verrazzano letter.¹ The intention to do so was known by Francis some time previously. He wrote on the 28th of June from Amboise, near Tours, to the Provençaux that he would march immediately to their relief;² and on the 2d of July he announced in a letter to his parliament: "I am going to Lyons to prevent the enemy from entering the kingdom, and I can assure you that Charles de Bourbon is not yet in France."³ He had left his residence at Blois and his capital, and was thus actually engaged in collecting his forces together, on the 8th of July, when the Verrazzano letter is dated. He did not reach Lyons until after the 4th of August, as is correctly stated in the Carli letter.⁴

The author of the Carli letter, whether the person he pretends to have been or not, asserts that news of the arrival of Verrazzano at Dieppe on his return from his voyage of discovery had reached Lyons, and that the navigator himself was expected soon to be in that city for the purpose of conferring with its merchants on the subject of the new countries which he had discovered, and had described in a letter to the king, a copy of which letter was enclosed. He thus explicitly declares not only that news of the discovery had reached Lyons, but that the letter to the king was known to the merchants at that place, and that a copy

---

[1] Letter of Bourbon. Dyer's Europe, 442.
[2] Sismondi, XVI, 216, 217.
[3] Gaillard, *Histoire de François Premier*, tom. III, 172 (Paris, 1769).
[4] Letter of Moncada in *Doc. ined. para la Hist. de España*, tom. XXIV, 403, and Letters of Pace to Wolsey in *State Papers of the reign of Henry VIII*, vol. IV, Part I, 589, 606.

of it was then actually in his possession and sent with his own. The result of the expedition was, therefore, notorious, and the letter had attained general publicity at Lyons, without the presence there of either Francis or Verrazzano.

This statement must be false. Granting that such a letter, as is ascribed to Verrazzano, had been written, it was impossible that this obscure young man at Lyons, hundreds of miles from Dieppe, Paris and Blois, away from the king and court and from Verrazzano, not only at a great distance from them all, but at the point to which the king was hastening, and had not reached, on his way to the scene of war in the southern portion of his kingdom, could have come into the possession of this document in less than a month after it purports to have been written for the king in a port far in the north, on the coast of Normandy. It obviously could not have been delivered to him personally by Verrazzano, who had not been at Lyons, nor could it have been transmitted to him by the navigator, who had not yet presented himself before the king, and could have had no authority to communicate it to any person. It was an official report, addressed to the king, and intended for his eye alone, until the monarch himself chose to make it public. It related to an enterprise of the crown, and eminently concerned its interests and prerogatives, in the magnitude and importance of the new countries; and could not have been sent by Verrazzano, without permission, to a private person, and especially a foreigner, without subjecting himself to the charge of disloyalty, if not of treason, which there is no other evidence to sustain. On the other hand it could not have been delivered by the king to this Carli. It is not probable, even if such a letter could have come into the hands of Francis, absent from his capital in the midst of warlike preparations, engaged in forming his army and *en route* for the scene of the invasion, that he could have given it any consideration. But if he had received it and considered its import, there was no official or other relation between him and Carli, or any motive for him to send it forward in advance of his coming to Lyons, to this young and obscure alien. There was no possibility, therefore, of Carli obtaining possession of a private copy of the letter through Verrazzano or the king.

The only way open to him, under the most favorable circumstances, would have been through some publicity, by proclamation or printing, by order of the king; in which case, it would have been given for the benefit of all his subjects. It is impossible that it could have been seen and copied by this young foreigner alone and in the city of Lyons, and that no other copies would have been preserved in all France. The idea of a publication is thus forbidden.

No alternative remains except to pronounce the whole story a fabrication. The Carli letter is untrue. It did not inclose any letter of Verrazzano of the character pretended. And as it is the only authority for the existence of any such letter, that falls with it.

III.

THE LETTER UNTRUE. I. NO VOYAGE OR DISCOVERY MADE FOR THE KING OF FRANCE, AS IT STATES.

All the circumstances relating to the existence of the Verrazzano letter thus prove that it was not the production of Verrazzano at the time and place it purports to have been written by him. We pass now to the question of its authenticity, embracing the consideration of its own statements and the external evidence which exists upon the subject.

The letter professes to give the origin and results of the voyage; that is, the agency of the king of France in sending forth the expedition, and the discoveries actually accomplished by it. In both respects it is essentially untrue. It commences by declaring that Verrazzano sailed under the orders and on behalf of the king of France, for the purpose of finding new countries, and that the account then presented was a description of the discoveries made in pursuance of such instructions. That no such voyage or discoveries were made for that monarch is clearly deducible from the history of France. Neither the letter, nor any document, chronicle, memoir, or history of any kind, public or private, printed or in manuscript, belonging to that period, or the reign of Francis I, who then bore the crown, mentioning or in any manner referring to it, or to the voyage and discovery, has ever been found in France; and neither Francis himself, nor any of his successors, ever acknowledged or in any manner recognized such discovery, or asserted under it any right to the possession of the country; but, on the contrary, both he and they ignored it, in undertaking colonization in that region by virtue of other discoveries made under their authority, or with their permission, by their subjects.

I. That no evidence of the Verrazzano discovery ever existed in France, is not only necessarily presumed from the circumstance that none has ever been produced, but is inferentially established by the fact that all the French writers and historians, who have had occasion to consider the subject, have derived their information in regard to it from the Italian so-called copies of the letter, and until recently from that in Ramusio alone. No allusion to the discovery, by any of them, occurs until several years after the work of Ramusio was published, when for the first time it is mentioned in the account written by Ribault, in 1563, of his voyage to Florida and attempted colonization at Port Royal in South Carolina, in the previous year. Ribault speaks of it very briefly, in connection with the discoveries of Sebastian Cabot and others, as having no practical results, and states that he had derived his information in regard to it, from what Verrazzano had written, thus clearly referring to the letter. He adds that Verrazzano made another voyage to America afterwards, "where at last he died." As Ramusio is the only authority known for the latter statement, it is evident that Ribault must have had his work before him, and consequently his version of the letter, when he prepared this account.[1] In the relation written by Laudoniere in 1566, but not printed until 1586, of all three of the expeditions sent out from France, for the colonization of the French protestants, mention is again made of the discoveries of Verrazzano. Laudoniere gives no authority, but speaks of them in terms which show that he made his compend from the discourse of the French captain of Dieppe, published by Ramusio in the same volume, in connection with the Verrazzano letter. He says that Verrazzano "was sent by King Francis the First and Madame the Regent, his mother, into these new countries." In thus associating the queen mother with the king in the prosecution of the enterprise Laudoniere commits the same mistake as is made in the discourse in that respect. Louise did not become regent until after the return of Verrazzano is stated to have taken place, and after both his letter and that of Carli are represented to have been written.[2] In adopting this error it is plain that Laudoniere must have taken it

---

[1] The original narrative of Ribault, in French, has never appeared in print. It was probably suppressed at the time for political reasons, as the colony was intended for the benefit of the protestants of France. It was, however, translated immediately into English and printed in 1563, under the following title: "The whole and true discoverye of Terra Florida &c never found out before the last year, 1562. Written in French by Captain Ribault &c and now newly set forthe in Englishe the XXX of May, 1563. Prynted at London, by Rowland Hall, for Thomas Hacket." This translation was reprinted by Hakluyt in his first work, *Divers Voyages*, in 1582; but was omitted by him in his larger collections, and the account by Laudoniere, who accompanied Ribault, of that and the two subsequent expeditions, substituted in its stead.

[2] The edict appointing Louise regent, was dated at Pignerol, the 17th of October, 1524, when Francis was *en route* for Milan. Isambert, *Recueil*, &c., tom. XII, part I, p. 230.

from the work of Ramusio, as the discourse of the French captain is found in no other place, and therefore used that work. He also speaks of the discovered country being called Francesca, as mentioned in the discourse.[1]

The Verrazzano discovery is referred to, for the first time, in any work printed in France, in 1570, in a small folio volume called the *Universal History of the World*, by François de Belleforest, a compiler of no great authority. In describing Canada, he characterizes the natives as cannibals, and in proof of the charge repeats the story, which is found in Ramusio only, of Verrazzano having been killed, roasted and eaten by them, and then proceeds with a short account of the country and its inhabitants, derived, as he states, from what Verrazzano had written to King Francis.[2] He does not mention where he obtained this account, but his reference to the manner in which Verrazzano came to his death, shows that he had consulted the volume of Ramusio. Five years later the same writer gave to the world an enlarged edition of his work, with the title of *The Universal Cosmography of the World*, in three ponderous folios, in which he recites, more at length, the contents of the Verrazzano letter, also without mentioning where he had found it, but disclosing nevertheless that it was in Ramusio, by his following the variations of that version, particularly in regard to the complexion of the natives represented to have been first seen, as they

---

[1] Basanier, *L'Histoire notable de la Floride*. (Paris, 1586), fol. 1 – 3. Hakluyt, III, p. 305. *Ramusio*, III, fol. 423. (Ed. 1556.)

[2] *L'Histoire Universelle du Monde*. Par François de Belleforest. (Paris 1570, fol. 253 – 4.)

will be hereafter explained.[1] This publication of Belleforest is the more important, because it is from the abstract of the Verrazzano letter contained in it, that Lescarbot, thirty-four years afterwards, took his account of the voyage and discovery, word for word, without acknowledgment.[2] The latter writer has accordingly been cited by subsequent authors as an original authority on the subject, among others by Bergeron,[3] and the commissioners of the king of France, in the controversy with his Britannic majesty

---

[1] *La Cosmographie Universelle de tout le Monde*, tom. II, part II, 2175 – 9. (Paris, 1575.)

[2] *Hist. de la Nouvelle France*, p. 27, et seq. (ed. 1609). In a subsequent portion of his history (p. 244) Lescarbot again refers incidentally to Verrazzano in connection with Jacques Cartier, to whom he attributes a preposterous statement, acknowledging the Verrazzano discovery. He states that in 1533 Cartier made known to Chabot, then admiral of France, his willingness "to discover countries, as the Spanish had done, in the West Indies, and as, nine years before, Jean Verrazzano (had done) under the authority of King Francis I, which Verrazzano, being prevented by death, had not conducted any colony into the lands he had discovered, and had only remarked the coast from about the *thirtieth* degree of the Terre-neuve, which at the present day they call Florida, as far as the *fortieth*. For the purpose of continuing his design he offered his services, if it were the pleasure of the king, to furnish him with the necessary means. The lord admiral having approved these words, represented then to his majesty, &c." Lescarbot gives no authority for this statement, made by him seventy-five years after the voyage of Cartier. It is absurd on its face and is contradicted by existing records of that voyage. No authority has ever confined the Verrazzano discovery within the limits here mentioned. Cartier is represented as saying to the admiral that in order to complete Verrazzano's design of carrying colonists to the country discovered by him, that is, within those limits, he would go himself, if the king would accept his services. The documents recently published from the archives of St. Malo, show that the voyage of Cartier proposed by Cartier, was for the purpose of passing through the straits of Belle Isle, in latitude 52°, far north of the northern limit of the Verrazzano discovery, according to either version of the letter, and not with a design of planting a colony, or going to any part of the Verrazzano explorations, much less to a point south of the fortieth degree. (Ramé, *Documents inédits sur Jacques Cartier et le Canada*, p. 3, Tross, Paris 1865.) Besides, neither in the commissions to Cartier, nor in any of the accounts of his voyages, is there the slightest allusion to Verrazzano.

[3] *Traicté des Navigations*, p. 103, § 15.

in relation to the limits of Acadia;[1] but, as this plagiarism proves, without reason. Charlevoix, with a proper discrimination, refers directly to Ramusio as the sole source from whence the account of the discovery is derived, as do the French writers who have mentioned it since his time, except M. Margry, who, in his recent work on the subject of French voyages, quotes from the Carli version. It is thus seen that no other authority is given by the French historians than one or other of the Italian versions.[2] It must, therefore, be regarded as confessed by them, that no

---

[1] *Memoirs des Commissaries du Roi*, &c., I, 29.

[2] André Thevet, who published a work with the title of *Cosmographie Universelle*, in two volumes, large folio, in rivalry apparently with Belleforest, and in the same year, 1575, is referred to sometimes as an authority on this subject. Speaking of the cruel disposition of the people of Canada, he mentions in illustration of it, the fate at their hands of some colonists whom Verrazzano took to that country. The fact is thus related by him in connection with this voyage, for which he gives no authority or indication of any. "Jean Verazze, a Florentine, left Dieppe, the *seventeenth of March*, one thousand five hundred and twenty-four, by command of King Francis, and coasted the whole of Florida as far as the thirty-fourth degree of latitude, and the three hundredth of longitude, and explored all this coast, and *placed there a number of people to cultivate it*, who in the end were all killed and massacred by this barbarous people" (fol. 1002 B.). This statement seems to justify what the President De Thou, the contemporary of Thevet, says of him, that he composed his books by putting "the uncertain for the certain, and the false for the true, with an astonishing assurance." (*Hist. Univ.*, tom. II, 651, Lond., 1734.) Thevet had published before this, in 1557, another book, called *Les Singularitez de la France Antarctique, autrement nommée Amerique*, in which he describes all the countries of America as far north as Labrador, and says that he ran up the coast to that region on his way home from Brazil, where he went in 1555, with Villegagnon. In this earlier work he makes no mention of Verrazzano; but does say that Jacques Cartier told him that he (Cartier) had made the voyage to America twice (fol. 148-9). It is thus evident that Thevet had not heard of Verrazzano in 1557, or he would necessarily have mentioned him, as he had the subject distinctly before him; and if he is to be believed in regard to his intimacy with Cartier, with whom he says he spent five months at his house in St. Malo (*Cos. Univ.*, fol. 1014, B.), and from whom he received much information, it is quite as clear that Cartier knew nothing of the Verrazzano discovery, or he would have mentioned it to Thevet.

original authority for the discovery has ever existed in France.

If any voyage had taken place, such as this is alleged to have been, it is morally impossible, in the state of learning and art at that time in France, and with the interest which must necessarily have attached to the discovery, that no notice should have been taken of it in any of the chronicles or histories of the country, and that the memory of it should not have been preserved in some of the productions of its press. According to the letter itself, it was one of the grandest achievements in the annals of discovery, and promised the most important results to France. It was an enterprise of her king, which had been successfully accomplished. There had been discovered a heathen land, nearly three thousand miles in extent, before unknown to the civilized world, and, therefore, open to subjugation and settlement; healthy, populous, fertile and apparently rich in gold and aromatics, and, therefore, an acquisition as great and valuable as any discovery made by the Spaniards or Portuguese, except that of Columbus. Silence and indifference in regard to such an event were impossible. Printing introduced long previously into the principal cities in France, had early in this reign reached its highest state of perfection, as the works issued from the presses of Henri Estienne and others attest. In 1521 twenty-four persons practiced the art in Paris alone.[1] The discoveries in the new world by other nations excited as much attention in France as they did in the other countries of Europe. The letters of Columbus and

---
[1] Didot in Harrisse *Bib Am. Vet.*, 189.

Vespucci, describing their voyages and the countries they had found, were no sooner published abroad than they were translated into French and printed in Paris. From 1515 to 1529 several editions of the Italian collection of voyages, known as the *Paesi novamente ritrovati*, containing accounts of the discoveries of Columbus, Cortereal, Cabral and Vespucci in America, and in 1532 the Decades of Peter Martyr, were translated and published in Paris, in the French language. Cartier's account of his voyage in 1535 – 6, undertaken by order of Francis, in which he discovered Canada, was printed in the same city in 1545, during the reign of that monarch. These publications abundantly prove the interest which was taken in France in the discoveries in the new world, and the disposition and efforts of the printers in the country at that time to supply the people with information on the subject; and also, that the policy of the crown allowed publicity to be given to its own maritime enterprises. Of the enlightened interest on the part of the crown in the new discoveries, a memorable instance is recorded, having a direct and important bearing upon this question. A few months only after the alleged return of Verrazzano, and at the darkest hour in the reign of Francis, when he was a captive of the emperor in Spain, Pigafetta, who had accompanied the expedition of Magellan and kept a journal of the voyage, presented himself at the court of France. Louise was then exercising the powers and prerogatives of her son, and guarding his interests and honor with maternal zeal. Pigafetta came to offer her a copy of the manuscript which he had prepared, and which told of the discovery of the newly discovered route to the Moluccas and Cathay. It was written in Italian; and the queen mother caused it to be translated into French by Antoine Fabre, and printed by Simon de Colines, the successor of Estienne. The book bears no date, but bibliographers assign it that of 1525, the year of the regency. Certain it is, it was printed in Paris during the life of Francis, as Colines, whose imprint it bears, died before the king. Thus by the instrumentality of the crown of France was the account of the discovery of Magellan, written by one who belonged to the expedition, first given to the world. It is not probable that the queen mother, exercising the regal power immediately after the alleged return of Verrazzano, would have left entirely unnoticed and unpublished an account of his discovery, so interesting to the subjects of the king and so glorious to France, and yet have caused to be put forth within his realm in its stead, the history of a like enterprise, redounding to the glory of the great rival and enemy of her son.[1]

II. Conclusive as the silence of the history of France is against the assertion that the Verrazzano voyage and discovery were made by direction of her king, the life of Francis is a complete denial of it. He was released from his captivity early in 1526, and lived and

---

[1] The little book of Pigafetta, a copy of which, by the kindness of Mrs. John Carter Brown, of Providence, is now in our hands, bears the title of *Le voyages et navigation faict par les Espaignols es Isles de Molucques, &c.* It is fully described by M. Harrisse in his *Bib. Vet. Am.* The concluding paragraph contains the statement that the manuscript was presented to the queen regent. Ramusio (vol. I, 346), mentions the fact that it was given by her to Fabre to be translated. The particulars are detailed by Amoretti *Primo Viaggio*, Introd. xxxvii. *Premier Voyage*, xliv.

reigned over France for more than twenty years afterwards, active in promoting the greatness of his kingdom; encouraging science and art among his people, and winning the title of father of letters; awake to whatever concerned his royal rights and prerogatives, and maintaining them with might and vigor abroad as well as at home; and willing and able to obtain and occupy new countries inhabited by the heathen. That he was not insensible to the advantages to his crown and realm of colonies in America, and not without the ability and disposition to prosecute discoveries there for the purpose of settlement, is proven by his actually sending out the expeditions of Jacques Cartier in 1534 and 1535 and Cartier and Roberval in 1541 – 2, for the purpose of exploring and developing the region beyond the gulf of St. Lawrence, through the icy way of the straits of Belle Isle, in latitude 52° N.

Yet he never recognized by word or deed the voyage or discovery of Verrazzano. If any one in France could have known of them, surely it would have been he who had sent forth the expedition. If Verrazzano were dead, when Francis returned to his kingdom, and the letter had miscarried and never come to his hands, the knowledge of the discovery still would have existed in the bosom of fifty living witnesses, who composed the crew, according to the story; and through them the results of the voyage would have been communicated to the king. But Verrazzano was not dead at that time, but was alive, as will appear hereafter, in 1527. There is good reason to believe that he was well known then to the royal advisers. One of the first acts of the king after his return from

Spain was to create Phillipe Chabot, Sieur de Brion, the admiral of France, whereby that nobleman became invested on the 23d of March, 1526, with the charge of the royal marine.[1] A document has recently been brought to light from among the manuscripts in the Bibliotheque Nationale in Paris, purporting to be an agreement made by Chabot in his official capacity, with Jean Ango, of Dieppe, and other persons, including Jehan de Varesam, for a voyage to the Indies with two vessels belonging to the king, and one to Ango, to be conducted by Varesam, as master pilot, for the purpose ostensibly of bringing back a cargo of spices.[2] This instrument has no date, but on its face belongs to Chabot's administration of the admiralty, and must, therefore, have been drawn up in the year 1526 or that of Verrazzano's death, in 1527. If it be genuine, it proves not only that Verrazzano was alive in that period, but was known to the admiral, and, consequently, that any services which he had previously rendered must have been in the possession of the crown. In either case, however, whether Verrazzano were dead or alive when Francis resumed his royal functions, there is no reason why the discovery, if it had ever taken place, should not have been known by him.

In sending forth the expeditions of Jacques Cartier and the joint expeditions of Cartier and Roberval, Francis not only showed his interest in the discovery of new countries, but he acted in perfect ignorance of the Verrazzano discovery. If it were known to him,

---

[1] Père Anselme, IV, 571.
[2] M. Margry. *Navigations Françaises*, p. 194. See Appendix.

upon what rational theory would he have attempted new voyages of discovery in a cold and inhospitable region, on an uncertain search, instead of developing what had been found for him? What could he have expected to have accomplished by the new expeditions that had not been already fully effected by Verrazzano? And, especially after the way to Canada was found out by Cartier, what was there more inviting in that unproductive quarter than was promised in the temperate climate, fertile soil, and mineral lands, which the Florentine had already discovered in his name, that he should have sent Cartier and Roberval to settle and conquer the newer land?[1]

With the failure of the expedition of Roberval, Francis abandoned the attempt to discover new countries, or plant colonies in America; but his successors, though much later, entered upon the colonization of New France. They inherited his rights, and while they acknowledged the discoveries of Cartier they discredited those ascribed to Verrazzano. Of the latter claim all of them must have known. The publication of Ramusio took place during the reign of Henry II, who died in 1559; but he made no

---

[1] The letters issued to Roberval have been recently published, for the first time, by M. Harrisse, from the archives of France, in his *Notes pour servir a l'histoire de la Nouvelle France*, p. 244, et seq. (Paris, 1872.) They are dated the 16th of February, 1540. Cartier's commission for the same service is dated in October, 1540. Charlevoix, misled probably by the letters granted by Henry IV to the Marquis de la Roche in 1598, in which the letters to Roberval are partially recited, asserts that Roberval is styled in them lord of Norumbega. The letters now published show that he was in error; and that France limited the authority of Roberval to the countries west of the gulf of St. Lawrence (Canada and Ochelaga), so far as any are named or described, and made no reference to Norumbega as a title of Roberval or otherwise. As the year commenced at Easter the date of Roberval's commission was in fact after that of Cartier.

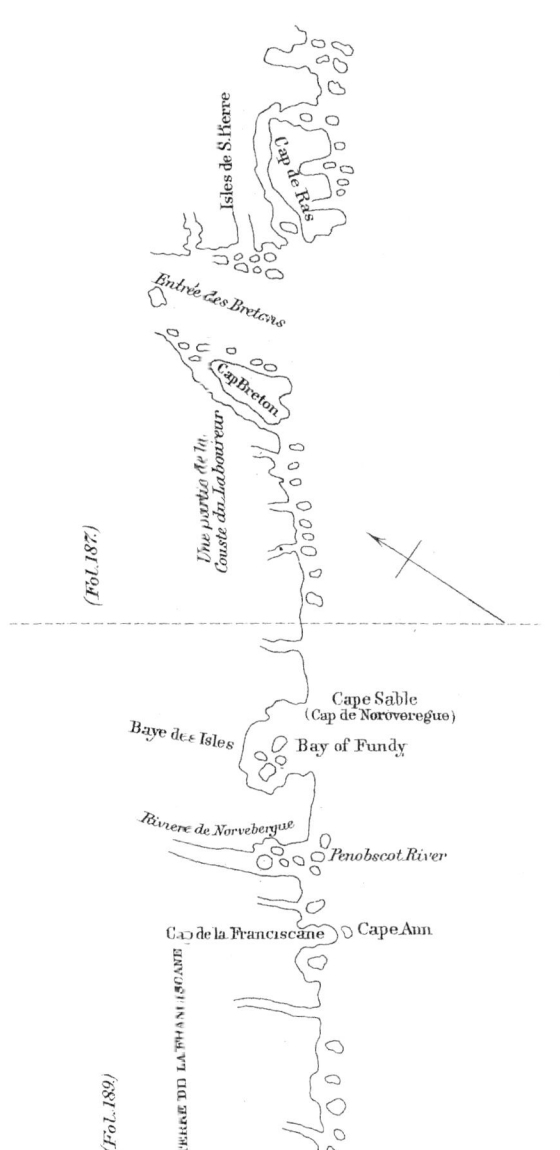

endeavor to plant colonies abroad. In 1577 and 1578, the first commissions looking to possessions in America north of Florida, were issued by Henry III, to the Marquis de la Roche, authorizing settlements in the *terres neufves* and the adjacent countries *newly* discovered, in the occupancy of barbarians, but nothing was done under them. In 1598, another grant was made to the same person by Henry IV, for the conquest of Canada, Hochelaga, Newfoundland, Labrador, the country of the river St. Lawrence, Norumbega, and other countries adjacent. This is the first document emanating from the crown, containing any mention of any part of the continent north of latitude 33° and south of Cape Breton.

Norumbega is the only country of those here enumerated which is included within those limits, and that did not become known through Verrazzano.[1] No

---

[1] Norumbega embraced the region of country extending from the land of the Bretons to the Penobscot, of which it was regarded as the Indian name. It was almost identical with what was subsequently called Acadia. It had become known at an early period through the French fishermen and traders in peltries, who obtained the name from the Indians and carried it home to France. It is described by Jean Alfonse, the chief pilot of Roberval, from an exploration which he made along the coast on the occasion of Roberval's expedition to Canada, in 1542. (Hakluyt, III, 239–40. MS. cosmography of Alfonse, in *Bib. Nat. of Paris*, fol. 185.) Alfonse states that he ran down the coast as far as a bay which he did not penetrate, in latitude 42°, between Norumbega and Florida, showing that Norumbega was considered as north of that parallel of latitude. He particularly describes it in the manuscript just cited, which Hakluyt had before him, as the ruttier of Alfonse which he publishes is found in that manuscript. It appears to have been written by Alfonse in 1544–5, which was shortly after his return from Canada with Roberval. The name of Norumbega is found in the discourse of the captain of Dieppe, written in 1539, and printed in third volume of Ramusio. This writer distinctly states that the name was derived from the natives. The description of the country and its inhabitants given by Alfonse, is important, as showing its extent, and alluding to the trade there in peltries thus early. It is found in the cosmography in connection with the ruttier before mentioned (fol. 187–8), and is as follows:

38   VERRAZZANO.

allusion is made, in these letters of de la Roche, to any previous exploration, although an erroneous recital,

"I say that the cape of S. Jehan, called Cape Breton and the cape of the Franciscane, are northeast and southwest, and take a quarter of east and west and there is in the route one hundred and forty leagues. And here makes a cape called the cape of *Noroveregue*. This said cape is at forty-five degrees of the height of the arctic pole. The said coast is all sandy land, low without any mountain. And along this coast there are several islands of sand and coast very dangerous, with banks and rocks. The people of this coast and of Cape Breton are bad people, powerful, great archers and live on fish and flesh. They speak, as it were, the same language as those of Canada, and are a great nation. And those of Cape Breton go and make war upon those of Newfoundland (*Terre Neufve*), where they fish. On no account would they save the life of a person when they capture him, if it be not a child or young girl, and are so cruel that if they find a man wearing a beard, they cut his limbs off and carry them to their wives and children, in order to be revenged in that matter. And there is among them much peltry of all animals. Beyond the cape of *Noroveregue* [Cape Sable] descends the river of the said Noroveregue which is about twenty-five leagues from the cape. The said river is more than forty leagues broad at its mouth, and extends this width inward well thirty or forty leagues, and is all full of islands which enter ten or twelve leagues into the sea, and it is very dangerous with rocks and reefs. The said river is at forty-two degrees of the height of the arctic pole. Fifteen leagues within this river is a city which is called *Norombergue*, and there are in it good people and *there is much peltry of all animals*. The people of the city are clothed with peltry, wearing mantles of martin. I suspect the said river enters into the river of Ochelaga, for it is salt more than forty league inward, according to what is said by the people of the city. The people use many words, which resemble Latin, and adore the sun; and are handsome and large men. The land of *Norobregue* is tolerably high. On the side on the west of the said city there are many rocks which run into the sea well fifteen leagues; and on the side towards the north there is a bay in which there is a little island which is very subject to tempest and cannot be inhabited."

Two sketches of the coast by Alfonse accompany this description, which are here reproduced united in one. The map in Ramusio (III, fol. 424–5), prepared by Gastaldi, shows the *Terra de Nurumbega*, of the same extent as here described, that is, from Cape Breton westerly to a river running north from the Atlantic and connecting with the St. Lawrence or river of Hochelaga. · Gastaldi, or Gastaldo, published previously an edition of *Ptolemy's Geography* (12mo., Venice, 1548), in which (map 56), Norumbega is similarly laid down, without the river running to the St. Lawrence. Norumbega was therefore a well defined district of country at that time.

The word was undoubtedly derived from the Indians, and is still in use by those of the Penobscot, to denote certain portions of that river. The missionary Vetromile, in his *History of the Abnakis* (New York, 1866), already alluded to, is made to a purpose of Francis I, in his commission to Roberval, to conquer the countries here indicated.[1] De la Roche made a miserable

---

observes (pp. 48 – 9): "Nolumbega means *a still-water between falls*, of which there are several in that river. At different times, travelling in a canoe along the Penobscot, I have heard the Indians calling those localities *Nolumbega*."

That the country did not become known through Verrazzano is evident from the letter, in which it is stated that he ran along the entire coast, from the harbor in which they remained fifteen days, one hundred and fifty leagues, easterly, that is from Cape Cod to the island of Cape Breton, without landing, and consequently without having any correspondence with the natives, so as to have acquired the same.

When in particular Alfonse ran along the Atlantic coast is not mentioned, though it is to be inferred that it was on the occasion of Roberval's expedition. There is nothing stated, it is true, to preclude the possibility of its having taken place on some other voyage previously. It could not have been afterwards, as the cosmography describing it was written in 1544 – 5. Some authors assert that Roberval despatched him towards Labrador with a view of finding a passage to the East Indies, without mentioning his exploration along Nova Scotia and New England. But Le Clerc, who seems to have been the author of this statement (*Premier Etablissement de la Foy dans la Nouvelle France*, I, 12 – 13. Paris, 1691), and who is followed by Charlevoix, also alleges that on the occasion of his exploration towards Labrador, he discovered the straits between it and Newfoundland, in latitude 52°, now known as the straits of Belle Isle, which is not correct. Jacques Cartier sailed through that passage in his first voyage to Canada, in 1534. Le Clerc either drew false inferences or relied upon false information. He probably derived his impression of the voyage to Labrador and the discovery of the straits by Alfonse, from a cursory reading of the cosmography of Alfonse, who describes these straits, but not as a discovery of his own.

In the printed work, called *Les voyages avantureux du Capitaine Jean Alphonce, Saintongeois*, which was first published in 1559, after the death of Alfonse, it is expressly stated that the river of Norumbega, was discovered by the Portuguese and Spaniards. Describing the great bank, he says that it runs from Labrador, " au nordest et suroest, une partie a oestsuroest, plus de huit cens lieues, et passe bien quatre vingts lieues de la terre neufue, et de la terre des Bretons trente ou quarante lieues. Et d'icy va tout au long de la coste jusques a la riviere du Norembergue, *qui est nouvellement descouverte par les Portugalois et Espagnols*." p. 53. We quote from an edition of the work not mentioned by the bibliographers (Brunet — Harrisse), printed at Rouen in 1602. This is almost a contemporary denial by a French author, whether Alfonse himself or a compiler, as it would rather appear, from his cosmography, of the Verrazzano discovery of this country.

[1] Lescarbot (ed. 1609), 434. Harrisse, *Notes de la Nouvelle France*, p. 243.

attempt to settle the island of Sable, a sand bank in the ocean, two degrees south of Cape Breton, with convicts taken from jails of France, but being repelled by storm and tempest, after leaving that island, from landing on the main coast, returned to France without any further attempt to colonize the country, and abandoning the poor malefactors on the island to a terrible fate.[1] There is therefore no acknowledgment, in the history of this enterprise, of the pretended discovery. The next act of the regal prerogative was a grant to the Sieur de Monts, by the same monarch in 1603, authorizing him to take possession of the country, coasts and confines of La Cadie, extending from latitude 40° N. to 46° N., that is, Nova Scotia and New England, the situation of which, it is alleged, De Monts understood from his previous voyages to the country.[2] This document also is utterly silent as to any particular discovery of the country; but it distinctly affirms that the foundation of the claim to this territory was the report of the captains of vessels, pilots, merchants and others, who had for a long time frequented the country and trafficked with its inhabitants. Accompanying these letters patent was a license to De Monts to trade with the natives of the St. Lawrence, and make settlements on that river. It was under these authorizations to De Monts exclusively, that all the permanent settlements of the

---

[1] The story is told by Lescarbot (p. 38, ed. 1609), which he subsequently embellished with some fabulous additions in relation to a visit to the island of Sable by Baron de Leri, in 1519 (Ed. 1611, p. 22), even before the date of the Verrazzano letter.

[2] Lescarbot (ed. 1609), 452 - 3. La Cadie, or Acadie, as it was for a long time afterwards known, appears for the first time on any chart on the map of Terra Nova, No. 56, in Gastaldi's Ptolemy, and is there called Lacadia.

French in Nova Scotia and Canada were effected, beyond which countries none were ever attempted by them, within the limits of the Verrazzano discovery, or any rights asserted on behalf of the French crown.

It is thus evident that the history of France and of her kings is utterly void on the subject of this discovery, without any legitimate cause, if it had ever taken place; and that the policy of the crown in regard to colonization in America has ever been entirely in repugnance to it. It is incredible, therefore, that any such could ever have taken place for Francis, or for France.

An important piece of testimony of an affirmative character, however, still exists, showing that the crown of France had no knowledge or appreciation of this claim. It comes from France, and, as it were, from Francis himself. It is to be found in the work of a French cartographer, a large and elaborately executed map of the world, which has been reproduced by M. Jomard, in his *Monuments of Geography*, under the title of *Mappemonde peinte sur parchemin par ordre de Henry II, roi de France*.[1] M. D'Avezac assigns it the date of 1542, which is five years before the death of Francis and accession of Henry to the throne.[2] But neither of these dates appears to be exactly correct; as upon that portion of the map representing Saguenay, the person of Roberval is depicted and his name in-

---

[1] *Les Monuments de la Géographie ou Receuil d'anciennes cartes, &c., en facsimile de la grandeur des originaux.* Par M. Jomard. No. XIX.

[2] *Inventaire et classement raisonné des "Monuments de la Géographie" publiés par M. Jomard de 1842 à 1862.* (*Communication de M. D'Avezac.*) Extrait du Bulletin de l'Academie des inscriptions et belles lettres. Séance du 30 Aout 1867, p. 7. *L'Année Géographique.* Sixiéme année (1867), pp. 543, 554.

scribed, evidently denoting his visit to that country, which did not take place until June, 1543.[1] No information, could possibly have arrived in France, to have enabled the maker of the map, to have indicated this circumstance upon it before the latter part of that year. On the other hand the arms of both the king and dauphin are repeatedly drawn in the decorated border of the map, showing that it was made, if not under the actual direction of Henry, at least while he was in fact discharging the functions of admiral of France, which he assumed after the disgrace of Chabot, in 1540, and continued to exercise until the death of Francis, in 1547. It therefore belongs to the period of 1543–7; and thus comes to us apparently impressed with an official character. It is the work of an accomplished French geographer, *during the reign of Francis*, and it, no doubt, represents not only the state of geographical knowledge in France at that time, but also all the knowledge possessed by Francis of this coast. Mr. Kohl expresses the opinion that it " is not only one of the most brilliant, but also one of the most exact and trustworthy pictures of the world which we have in the first part of the sixteenth century. It gives accurately all that was known of the world in 1543, especially of the ocean, and the outlines of the coasts of different countries." He adds, " the author of the map must have been a well instructed, intelligent and conscientious man. Where the coasts of a country are not known to him, he so designates them. For his representations of countries recently discovered and

---

[1] Hakluyt, III, 242.

NO DISCOVERY MADE FOR FRANCIS I. 43

already known, he had before him the best models and originals."[1] Yet notwithstanding the thorough knowledge of the subject displayed by this cartographer, his French nationality, and the contemporariness of his labors with the reign of Francis, " no evidence," as Mr. K. further observes, " appears that the report or chart of the French commander, Verrazzano, had been used in constructing this chart." On the contrary, the line of coast from Cape St. Roman in South Carolina to Cape Breton is copied from the Spanish map of Ribero, with the Spanish names translated into French.[2] Many other names occur within the same distance, which are found on other Spanish charts since that time, and some which were probably taken from Spanish charts not now known.[3] Thus within the limits mentioned, embracing the exploration of Gomez no designation occurs connecting the coast with Verrazzano.[4] From Cape Breton easterly and northerly along the coast of Newfoundland the discoveries of the Normand and Bretons and the Portuguese, and in the river and

---

[1] *Discovery of Maine*, 351-4.

[2] Thus R. del principe, R. del espiritu santo, B. de Santa Maria (the Chesapeake) Playa, C. de S. Juan, R. de St. iago, C. de Arenas (Cape Henlopen), B. de S. Christoval (the Delaware), B. de S. Antonio (the Hudson), R. de buena Madre, S. Juan Baptista, Arcipelago de Estevan Gomez, Montanas, and R. de la buelta, on the map of Ribero, become on the French map, R. du Prince, R. du St. Esprit, B. de Sa. Marie, Les playnes, C. St. Jean, St. Jacques, C. des Sablons, G. de St. Christofle, R. de St. Anthoine, R. de bonne Mere, Baye de St. Jean Baptiste, Arcipel de Estienne Gomez, Les Montaignes and R. de Volte.

[3] Of this class are the R. de Canoes, R. Seche, Playne, Coste de Dieu, R. d'Arbres, which, on the map XII, of the Munich Atlas, said to have been taken from the map of the Spanish cosmographer, Alonzo de Santa Cruz, are given, R. de Canoas, R. Seco, Terra llana, Costa de Diego, R. d Arvoredos.

[4] The name of Avorobagra, on the west side of the great bay, is found in place of C. de Muchas illas of the Ribero map. This is supposed to have been intended for Norumbega.

gulf of St. Lawrence, those of Jacques Cartier, are shown by the names. The whole coast claimed by the letter is thus assigned to other parties than Verrazzano. The logical maxim, *expressio unius est exclusio alterius*, must here apply. The expression of the Spanish discoveries, at least exclude those of Verrazzano; demonstrating almost to a moral certainty that the latter could never have been performed for the king of France. The author of this map, whether executing it under official responsibility or upon his own account, would not have ascribed, or dared to ascribe, to a foreign nation, much less to a rival, the glory which belonged to his own sovereign, then living, whose protection he enjoyed.

ARMS OF THE DAUPHIN, AFTERWARDS HENRY II.
From the *Mappemonde* published by M. Jomard.

IV.

I. Misrepresentations in regard to the Geography of the Coast. The Chesapeake. The Island of Louise. Massachusetts Bay.

In pursuing its main object of making known the discovery, the letter ventures upon certain statements which are utterly inconsistent with an actual exploration of the country. The general position and direction of the coast are given with sufficient correctness to indicate the presence there of a navigator; but its geographical features are so meagrely and untruthfully represented, as to prove that he could not have been the writer. The same apparent inconsistency exists as to the natural history of the country. Some details are given in regard to the natives, which correspond with their known characteristics, but others are flagrantly false. The account is evidently the work of a person who, with an imperfect outline of the coast, by another hand, before him, undertook to describe its hydrographical character at a venture, so far as he deemed it prudent to say anything on the subject; and to give the natural history of the country, in the same way, founded on other accounts of parts of the new world. The actual falsity of the statements alluded to is, at all events, sufficient to justify the rejection of the whole story. So far as they relate to the littoral, they are now to be considered.

In general, the geography of the coast is very indefinitely described. Of its latitudes, with the exception of the landfall and termination of the exploration, which are fixed also by other means, and are necessary to the ground work of the story, only a single one is mentioned. The particular features of the coast are for the most part unnoticed. Long distances, embracing from two hundred to six hundred miles each, are passed over with little or no remark. Islands, rivers, capes, bays, and other land or seamarks, by which navigators usually describe their progress along an unknown coast, are almost entirely unmentioned. For a distance of over two thousand miles, adopting the narrowest limits possible assigned to the discovery, only one island, one river, and one bay are attempted to be described, and not a single cape or headland is referred to. No name is given to any of them, or to any part of the coast, except the one island which is named after the king's mother. It was the uniform practice of the Catholic navigators of that early period, among whom, according to the import of the letter, Verrazzano was one, to designate the places discovered by them, by the names of the saints whose feasts were observed on the days they were discovered, or of the festivals of the church celebrated on those days; so that, says Oviedo, it is possible to trace the course of any such explorer along a new coast by means of the church calendar. This custom was not peculiar to the countrymen of that historian. It was observed by the Portuguese and also by the French, as the accounts of the voyages of Jacques Cartier attest. But nothing of the kind appears here. These omissions of the ordinary and accustomed practices of voyagers are suspicious, and of themselves sufficient to destroy all confidence in the narrative. But to proceed to what is actually stated in regard to the coast.

Taking the landfall to have occurred, as is distinctly claimed, at latitude 34°, which is a few leagues north of Cape Fear in North Carolina, and which is fixed with certainty, for the purposes of the letter, at that point by the estimate of the distance they ran northerly along the coast before it took an easterly direction, the discovery must be regarded as having commenced somewhat south of Cape Roman in South Carolina, being the point where the fifty leagues terminated which they ran along the coast, in the first instance, south of the landfall. It is declared that from thence, for two hundred leagues, to the Hudson river, as it will appear, there was not a single harbor in which the Dauphine could ride in safety.[1] The size of this craft is not mentioned, but it is said she carried only fifty men, though manned as a corsair. Judging from the size of the vessels used at that time on similar expeditions, she was small. The two which composed the first expedition of Jacques Cartier carried sixty men and were each of about sixty tons burden. The Carli letter, which must be assumed to express the idea of the writer on the subject, describes her as a caravel; which was a vessel of light draught adapted to enter shallow rivers and harbors and to double unknown capes where shoals might have formed, and was therefore much used by the early navigators of the

---

[1] A league, according to the Verrazzano letter, consisted of four miles; and a degree, of 15.625 leagues or 62½ miles.

new world.[1] Columbus chose two caravels, out of the three vessels with which he made his first voyage; and the third one, which was larger than either of the caravels, was less than one hundred tons. The Dauphine is therefore to be considered, from all the representations in regard to her, of less than the latter capacity, and as specially adapted to the kind of service in which she is alleged to have been engaged. In running north from their extreme southerly limit, they must have passed the harbor of Georgetown in South Carolina, and Beaufort in North Carolina, in either of which the vessel could have entered, and in the latter, carrying seventeen feet at low water and obtaining perfect shelter from all winds.[2] But if they really had been unable to find either of them, it is impossible that they should not have discovered the Chesapeake, and entered it, under the alleged circumstances of their search. That it may be seen what exactly is the statement of the letter in regard to this portion of the coast, it is here given in its own terms. Having represented the explorers as having reached a point fifty leagues north of the landfall, which would have carried them north of Hatteras, but still on the coast of North Carolina, their movements over the next four hundred miles north are disposed of in the following summary manner: "After having remained here," (that is, at or near Albemarle,) "three days riding at anchor on the coast, as we could find no harbor, we determined to depart and coast along the shore to the

---

[1] *Le Moyen Age et la Renaissance.* Tome Second. *Marine*, par M A. Jal. fol. v. (Paris 1849.)

[2] Blunt's *American Coast Pilot*, p. 359 (19th edition.)

northeast, keeping sail on the vessel *only by day*, and coming to anchor by night. After proceeding one hundred leagues we found a *very pleasant situation among some steep hills, through which a very large river, deep at its mouth, forced its way to the sea.*" There can be no mistake in regard to the portion of the coast here intended. Upon leaving this river they found that the coast stretched, it is stated, as will presently appear, in an *easterly* direction. A stream coming from the hills, its situation at the bend of the coast, its latitude as fixed by that of the port which, after leaving it, they found in nearly the same parallel and which is placed in 41° 40', all point distinctly to the embouchure of the Hudson at the highlands of Navesink as the termination of the hundred leagues. Within this distance the Chesapeake empties into the sea.

The explorers were not only in search of a harbor for the purpose of recruiting, but they were seeking, as the great end of the voyage, a passage to Cathay, rendering, therefore, every opening in the coast an object of peculiar interest and importance. They were sailing with extreme caution and observation, in the day-time only, and constantly in sight of land. The bay of the Chesapeake is the most accessible and capacious on the coast of the United States. It presents an opening into the sea of twelve miles from cape to cape, having a broad and deep channel through which the largest ships of modern times, twenty times or more the tonnage of the Dauphiny, may enter and find inside of Cape Henry ample and safe anchorage.[1] That an actual explorer could not have failed to have discovered

---

[1] Blunt's *American Coast Pilot*, p. 340.

this bay and found a secure harbor at that time, is shown by the account of the expedition, which the Adelantado, Pedro Menendez, of infamous memory, despatched under the command of Pedro Menendez Marquez, for the survey of this coast in 1573; when the means and facilities of navigators for exploration were not different from what existed at the date of the Verrazzano voyage. Menendez Marquez was the first to enter the Chesapeake after Gomez, who gave it the name of the bay of Santa Maria.[1] Barcia thus summarizes the result of the expedition, so far as it relates to this bay.

"Pedro Menendez Marquez, governor of Florida for his uncle the Adelantado reduced many Indians to obedience and took possession of the provinces particularly in the name of the king, in the presence of Rodrigo de Carrion, notary of the government of Santa Elena. Afterwards, he, being a great seaman, inasmuch as he had formerly been admiral of the fleet, as Francisco Cano relates, *Lib.* 3, *de la Histor. de las Ordenes Militares, fol.* 184, went, by order of the Adelantado, to explore the coast, which exploration commenced at the cape of the Martyrs, and the peninsula Tequesta [point of Florida], where the coast begins to run north and south, at the outlet of the Bahama channel, and extended along the coast to beyond the harbor and bay of Santa Maria, which is three leagues wide and which is entered towards the northwest; and within it are many rivers and harbors where, on both sides of it, they can anchor. At the entrance, near the shore, on the south, there are from nine to thirteen fathoms of water, and on the north from five to seven. Two leagues outside, in the sea, the depth is the same, north and south, but more sandy than inside. Going through the channel there are from nine to thirteen fathoms; and in the harbor about fifteen, ten and six fathoms were found in places where the lead was thrown." "The bay of Santa Maria is in thirty-seven degrees and a half.[2]"

---

[1] This name occurs on the map of Ribero on this part of the coast, which establishes its application by Gomez; but its position is evidently misplaced and carried too far south.
[2] *Ensayo Chronologico*, pp. 146, 8.

COAST GEOGRAPHY MISREPRESENTED. 51

To ignore the existence of this great bay, the most important hydrographical feature of our coast, as Verrazzano, according to the letter, does, and to pretend that no harbor could be found there, in which the diminutive Dauphiny could lie, is, under the circumstances under which this exploration is alleged to have been conducted, to admit that he was never on that part of the coast.

Suddenly leaving the river of the hills, in consequence of an approaching storm, they continued their course directly east for a distance of ninety-five leagues, passing in sight of the island and arriving finally at the bay, which are the only ones described, and that very briefly, in the whole voyage along the coast.

"Weighing anchor," reads the letter, "we sailed eighty leagues *towards the east*, as the coast stretched in that direction, and *always in sight of it*. At length we discovered an island of triangular form, about ten leagues from the main land, in size about equal to the island of Rhodes, having many hills covered with trees and well peopled, judging from the great number of fires which we saw all around its shores; we gave it the name of your majesty's illustrious mother. *We did not land there*, as the weather was unfavorable, but proceeded to another place, fifteen leagues distant from the island, where we found a very excellent harbor. * * * This land is situated in the parallel of Rome, being 41° 40' of north latitude. It looks towards the south, on which side the harbor is half a league broad; afterwards, upon entering it between the east and the north it extends twelve leagues,[1] and then enlarging itself it forms a very large bay, twenty leagues in circumference, in which are five small islands of great fertility and beauty, covered with large and lofty trees. Among these islands any fleet, however large, might ride safely, without fear of tempests or other dangers. Turning towards the

---

[1] A slight correction of the translation of Dr. Cogswell, which is the one we have adopted, here becomes necessary. It reads: "upon entering it the extent between the east (misprinted coast), and north is twelve leagues." The text is, "entrando in quello infra oriente e settentrione s'estende leghe XII."

south, at the entrance of the harbor on both sides there are very pleasant hills and many streams of clear water which flow down to the sea. In the midst of the entrance, there is a rock of freestone, formed by nature and suitable for the construction of any kind of machine or bulwark for the defence of the harbor."

This island is a mere fancy; none such exists any where upon this coast. The distance which they thus ran easterly, of eighty leagues, would have carried them more than an hundred miles into the ocean beyond Cape Cod. That distance, however, may be regarded only as approximate, because they possessed no means of determining longitude with accuracy, and therefore this, like all statements in the letter, of distances running east and west, is to be considered an estimate only, formed from the circumstances attending the sailing of the vessel, and liable to serious error. But the island and bay were objects of actual observation, and are therefore to be regarded as they are described. After leaving Long Island, which forms the coast in an easterly direction for a little over an hundred miles from the Hudson, only three islands occur, except some insignificant ones and the group of the Elizabeth islands all near the shore, in the entire distance to the easterly shore of Cape Cod, when the coast turns directly north. They are all three somewhat of a triangular shape, and in that respect are equally entitled to consideration in connection with the description of the island of Louise, but are all incompatible with it in other particulars. Louise is represented as being a very large island, equal in size to the famous island of Rhodes, which has an area of four hundred square miles, and as being situated ten leagues distant from the main land. The first of the three islands met with, eastward of Long Island, is Block island. It contains less than twenty square miles of territory and lies only three leagues from the land; and thus both by its smallness and position cannot be taken as the island of Louise. It has, however, been so regarded by some writers, because on the main land, about five leagues distant, are found Narraganset bay and the harbor of Newport, which, it is imagined, bear some resemblance to the bay and harbor which the explorers entered fifteen leagues beyond the island of Louise, and which cannot be elsewhere found.

But Narraganset bay does not correspond in any particular with the bay described in the letter, except as to its southern exposure and its latitude, and as to them it has no more claim to consideration than Buzzard's bay, three leagues further east, and in other respects not so much. Newport harbor, several miles inside of Narraganset bay, faces the north and west, and not the south. The whole length of that bay, including the harbor of Newport from the ocean to Providence river, is less than five leagues, and its greatest breadth not more than three. But the harbor described in the letter first as extending twelve leagues and then enlarging itself, formed a large bay of twenty leagues in circumference. The two, it is clear, are essentially unlike. The great rock rising out of the sea at the entrance of the harbor, has no existence in this bay or harbor. Narraganset bay, therefore, affords no support to the idea that Block island, or any other, is the island of Louise. Martha's Vineyard, the second of the three islands before mentioned, is the largest of them, but it contains only one hundred and twenty square miles of land, and is within two leagues of the main land. Nantucket, the last of the three, is less than half the size of Martha's Vineyard, and is about thirty miles from Cape Cod, the nearest part of the continent. From neither of them is any harbor to be reached corresponding with that mentioned in the letter. It is incontrovertible, therefore, that there is neither island nor bay on this coast answering the description. It is not difficult to perceive that the island of Louise was a mere invention and artifice on the part of the writer to give consistency to the pretension that the voyage originated with Francis. This island is the only one of which particular mention is made in the whole exploration. Yet it was not visited or seen except, in sailing by it, at a distance. Its pretended hills and trees disclosed nothing of its character; and, under such circumstances, its alleged dimensions were all that could have entitled it to such particular notice and made it worthy of so exalted a designation; and to those no island on this coast has any claim.

There is little room to doubt from the description itself, and the fact will be confirmed by other evidence hereafter, that the bay intended to be described was the great bay of Massachusetts and Maine terminating in the bay of Fundy. It is represented as making an offset in the coast of twelve leagues towards the north, and then swelling into an enclosed bay beyond, of twenty leagues in circumference, indicating those bays, in their form. The distances, it is true, do not conform to those belonging to that part of the coast; but it is to be borne in mind that they may have been taken, according to the only view which can reconcile

COAST GEOGRAPHY MISREPRESENTED. 55

the contradictions of the letter, from an imperfect delineation of the coast by another hand. The identity of the two is, however, proven, without recourse to this explanation, by the description of the coast beyond, which is given as follows:

"Having supplied ourselves with every thing necessary, we departed, on the sixth[1] of May, from this port [where they had remained fifteen days] and *sailed one hundred and fifty leagues, keeping so near to the coast as never to lose it from our sight;* the nature of the country appeared much the same as before, but the *mountains* were a little higher and all in appearance *rich in minerals.* We did *not stop to land*, as the weather was very favorable for pursuing our voyage, and the country presented no variety. *The shore stretched to the east,* and fifty leagues beyond more to the north, where we found a more elevated country full of very thick woods of fir trees, cypresses and the like, indicative of a cold climate. The people were entirely different from the others we had seen, whom we had found kind and gentle, but these were so rude and barbarous that we were unable by any signs we could make to hold communication with them."

This is all that is mentioned in regard to the entire coast of New England and Nova Scotia, embracing a distance of eight hundred miles according to this computation, but in fact much more. It is here stated, however, distinctly, that from the time of leaving the harbor, near the island of Louise, they kept close to the land, which ran in an *easterly* direction, and *constantly in sight of it,* for one hundred and fifty leagues. This they could not have done if that harbor were on any part of the coast, west of Massachusetts bay. If they sailed from Narraganset bay, or Buzzard's bay, or from any harbor on that coast, east of Long Island, they would in the course of twenty

---

[1] According to the *Archivio Storico Italiano*, and not the *fifth,* as given in *N. Y. Hist. Coll.*

leagues at the furthest, in an easterly direction, have reached the easterly extremity of the peninsula of Cape Cod, and keeping close to the shore would have been forced for one hundred and fifty miles, in a northerly and west of north direction, and thence along the coast of Maine northeasterly a further distance of one hundred and fifty miles, and been finally locked in the bay of Fundy. It is only by running from Cape Sable along the shores of Nova Scotia that this course and distance, in sight of the land, can be reconciled with the actual direction of the coast; and this makes the opening between Cape Cod and Cape Sable the large bay intended in the letter. But this opening of eighty leagues in width, could never have been seen by the writer of it; and nothing could more conclusively prove his ignorance of the coast, than his statements that from the river among the hills, for the distance of ninety-five leagues easterly to the harbor in 41°40' N. and from thence for a further distance of one hundred and fifty leagues, also *easterly*, the land was always in sight.

CAPE HENRY AND ENTRANCE INTO THE CHESAPEAKE.

Lighthouse, with lantern 129 feet above the sea, bearing W. N. W. ½ W., three leagues distant.

V.

III. Cape Breton and the Southerly Coast of Newfoundland, here claimed to have been discovered,
were known previously. Perversion of the Text of
the Letter by Ramusio.

By the two courses and distances last mentioned, the explorers are brought first to the island of Cape Breton, and then to the cape of that name, where the coast first takes a decided turn, from its easterly direction, to the north, and forms the westerly side of the strait leading into the gulf of St. Lawrence. This cape, according to the letter, is distant easterly one hundred and fifty, and fifty, leagues from the harbor in the great bay, distances which, for reasons already mentioned, are to be regarded as estimates only, but which taken exactly would have carried them beyond Cape Race in Newfoundland. They are to be considered, however, as properly limited to the turn of the coast before mentioned, as that is a governing circumstance in the description. Beyond this point, north, and east, the letter presents the claim to the discovery in another aspect. Thus far it relates to portions of the coast confessedly unknown before its date. But from Cape Breton, in latitude 46° N. to latitude 50° N. on the east side of Newfoundland, it pretends to the discovery of parts, which were in fact already known; and it makes this claim under circumstances which prove it was so known by the writer, if the letter were written as pretended. Having described their attempts at intercourse with the natives at Cape Breton, the narrative concludes the description of the coast with the following paragraph.

" Departing from thence, we kept along the coast, steering northeast, and found the country more pleasant and open, free from woods, and distant in the interior, we saw lofty mountains but none which extended to the shore. Within fifty leagues we discovered thirty-two islands, all near the main land, small and of pleasant appearance, but high and so disposed as to afford excellent harbors and channels, as we see in the Adriatic gulf, near Illyria and Dalmatia. We had no intercourse with the people, but we judge that they were similar in nature and usages to those we were last among. After sailing between east and north one hundred and fifty leagues *more*, and finding our provisions and naval stores nearly exhausted, we took in wood and water, and determined to return to France, having discovered (*avendo discoperto*) VII,[1] that is, 700 leagues of unknown lands."

The exact point at which they left the coast, and to which their discovery is thus stated to have extended, is given in the cosmography which follows the narrative, in these words:

" In the voyage which we have made by order of your majesty, in addition to the 92 degrees we ran towards the west from our point of departure (the Desertas) before we reached land in the latitude of 34, we have to count 300 leagues which we ran northeastwardly, and 400 nearly east along the coast before we reached the 50*th parallel of north latitude*, the point where we turned our course from the shore towards home. *Beyond this point the Portuguese had already sailed as far as the Arctic Circle, without coming to the termination of the land.*"

---

[1] "The MS. has erroneously and uselessly the repetition VII, that is, 700 leagues." *Note*, by M. Arcangeli. It is evident that VII is mistakenly rendered 502 in the transcription used by Dr. Cogswell.

PRIOR KNOWLEDGE OF THE NORTHERN COAST. 59

That this latitude must be taken as correctly determined follows from the representation of the letter, that they took daily observations of the sun and made a record of them, so that no material error could have occurred and remained unrectified for over twenty-four hours; and from the presumption that they were as capable of calculating the latitude as other navigators of that period, sent on such purposes by royal authority, like Jacques Cartier, whose observations, as the accounts of his voyage to this region show, never varied half a degree from the true latitude. The fiftieth parallel strikes the easterly coast of Newfoundland three degrees north of Cape Race, and to that point the exploration of Verrazzano is therefore to be regarded as claimed to have been made.[1]

This intention is made positively certain by the remark which follows the statement of the latitude, that "beyond this point the Portuguese had already sailed as far north as the Artic circle without coming to the termination of the land." The exploration of the Portuguese here referred to, and as far as which that of Verrazzano is carried, was made by Gaspar Cortereal in his second voyage, when according to the letter of Pasqualigo the Venetian embassador, he sailed from Lisbon on a course between west and northwest, and struck a coast along which he ran from six to seven hundred miles, "without finding the end."[2] No other exploration along this coast by the Portuguese, tending to

[1] Damiam de Goes, *Chronica do felicissimo rei Dom Emanuel* parte I. c. 66. (Fol., Lisboa, 1566.)
[2] *Paesi novamente ritrovati.* Lib. sexto. cap. CXXXI. Venice, 1521. A translation into English of Pasqualigo's letter, which is dated the 19th of October, 1501, is given in the memoir of Sebastian Cabot, p. 235-6.

the Arctic circle is known to have taken place before the publication of the Verrazzano letter. The first voyage of Cortereal, was, according to the description of the people given by Damiam de Goes, among the Esquimaux, whether on the one side or the other of Davis straits it is unnecessary here to inquire, as the Esquimaux are not found south of 50° N. latitude. The land along which he ran in his second voyage, was, according to the same historian, distinctly named after him and his brother, who shared his fate in a subsequent voyage. It is so called on several early printed maps on which it is represented as identical with Newfoundland. It appears first on a map of the world in the Ptolemy of 1511 edited by Bernardus Sylvanus of Eboli, and is there laid down as extending from latitude 50° N. to 60° N. with the name of Corte Real or Court Royal, latinized into *Regalis Domus*.[1] The length of the coast, corresponds with the description of Pasqualigo, and its position with the latitude assigned by the Verrazzano letter for their exploration. Its direction is north and south. There can be no question therefore as to the pretension of the Verrazzano letter to the discovery of the coast by him, actually as far north as the fiftieth parallel.

That it is utterly unfounded, so far as regards that portion of the coast lying east and north of Cape Breton, that is, from 46° N. latitude to 50° N., embracing a distance of five hundred miles according to actual measurement, or eight hundred miles according

---

[1] *Claudii Ptholemaei Alexandrini liber geographiae, cum tabulis et universali figura et cum additione locorum quae a recentioribus reperta sunt diligenti cura emendatus et impressus.* (Fol., Venetiis, 1511.)

to the letter, is proven by the fact, that it had all been known and frequented by Portuguese and French fishermen, for a period of twenty years preceding the Verrazzano voyage. The Portuguese fisheries in Newfoundland must have commenced shortly after the voyages of the brothers Cortereaes in 1501-2, as they appear to have been carried on in 1506, from a decree of the king of Portugal published at Leiria on the 14th of October in that year, directing his officers to collect tithes of fish which should be brought into his kingdom from Terra Nova;[1] and Portuguese charts belonging to that period, still extant, show both the Portuguese and French discoveries of this coast. On a map (No. 1, of the Munich atlas,) of Pedro Reinel, a Portuguese pilot, who entered the service of the king of Spain at the time of fitting out Magellan's famous expedition, Terra Nova, and the land of Cape Breton are correctly laid down, as regards latitude, though not by name. On Terra Nova the name of C. Raso, (preserved in the modern Cape Race) is applied to its southeasterly point, and other Portuguese names, several of which also still remain, designating different points along the easterly coast of Newfoundland, and a Portuguese banner, as an emblem of its discovery by that nation, are found. Another Portuguese chart, belonging to the period when the country between Florida and Terra Nova was unknown (No. 4 of the same atlas) delineates the land of Cape Breton, not then yet known to be an island, in correct relation with the Bacalaos, accompanied by a legend that it was discovered by

---

[1] *Memorias Economicas da academia Real das Sciencias de Lisboa*, tom. III, 393.

the Bretons.[1] The French authorities are more explicit. The particular parts of this coast discovered by the Normands and Bretons with the time of their discovery, and by the Portuguese, are described in the discourse of the French captain of Dieppe, which is found in the collection of Ramusio. This writer states that this land from Cape Breton to Cape Race was discovered by the Bretons and Normands in 1504, and from Cape Race to Cape Bonavista, seventy leagues north, by the Portuguese, and from thence to the straits of Belle Isle by the Bretons and Normands; and that the country was visited in 1508 by a vessel from Dieppe, commanded by Thomas Aubert, who brought back to France some of the natives. This statement in regard to the Indians is confirmed by an account of them, which is given in a work, printed in Paris at the time, establishing the fact of the actual presence of the Normands in Newfoundland in that year, by contemporaneous testimony of undoubted authority.[2]

---

[1] *Atlas zur entdeckungsgeschichte Amerikas. Herausgegeben von Friedrich Kunstmann, Karl von Spruner, Georg M. Thomas. Zu den Monumenta Sæcularia der K. B. Akademie der Wissenschaften,* 28 Maerz, 1859. Munchen.

[2] *Eusebii Chronicon,* continued by Joannes Multivallis of Louvain, (Paris 1512) fol. 172.

We give here, a translation of the interesting passage referred to in the text, from this volume, which came from the celebrated press of Henri Estienne.

"*An Salutis,* 1509. Seven savages were brought to Rouen with their garments and weapons from the island they call Terra Nova. They are of a dark complexion, have thick lips and wear marks on their faces extending along their jaws, from the ear to the middle of the chin *like small livid veins.* Their hair is black and coarse like a horse's mane. They have no beard, during their lives, or hairs of puberty. Nor have they hair on any part of their persons, except the head and eye-brows. They wear a girdle on which is a small skin to cover their nakedness. They form their speech with their lips. No religion. *Their boat is of bark* and a man may carry it with one hand on his shoulders. Their weapons are bows drawn with a string made of the intestines or sinews of animals, and

That the French and especially the Normands had soon afterwards resorted to Newfoundland for the purpose of taking fish, and were actually so engaged there at the time of the Verrazzano voyage, is evident from the letter of John Rut, who commanded one of the ships sent out on a voyage of discovery by Henry VIII of England in 1527. That voyager states that, driven from the north by the ice, he arrived at St. Johns in Newfoundland on the third of August in that year, and found there eleven Normand, one Breton and two Portuguese vessels, "all a fishing."[1] This was at a single point on the coast, and in latitude 47° 30' N.; and so large a number of vessels there denotes a growth of many years, at that time, of those fisheries.

---

arrows pointed with stone or fish-bone. Their food consists of roasted flesh, their drink is water. Bread, wine and the use of money they have none. They go about naked or dressed in the skins of bears, deer, seals and similar animals. Their country is in the parallel of the seventh climate, more under the west than France is above the west." *Plus sub occidente quam Gallica regio supra occidentem.* By "west" here is meant the meridional line, from which longitude was calculated at that time, through the Island of Ferro, the most westerly of the Canary islands, and the idea here intended to be conveyed is that the country of these Indians was further on this side than France was on the other side, of that line.

This description, as well as the name, Terra Nova, indicates the region of Newfoundland as the place from whence these Indians were taken. According to the tables of Pierre d'Ailly the seventh climate commences at 47° 15' N. and extends to 50° 30' N. beginning where the longest day of the year is 15 hours and 45 minutes long. (*Imago Mundi*, tables prefixed to the first chapter.) This embraces the greater part of the southerly and easterly coasts of Newfoundland. The practice of tattooing their faces in lines across the jaws, as here described, was common to all the tribes of this northern coast, the Nasquapees of Labrador, the red Indians of Newfoundland and the Micmacs of Cape Breton and Nova Scotia. It was from the use of red ochre for this purpose that the natives of Newfoundland obtained their designation of red Indians. The Micmacs used blue and other colors; hence it would appear from the circumstance of the marks upon these Indians being livid (*lividæ*) or blue, like veins, that they belonged to the tribes of Cape Breton. (Hind's Labrador II, 97–110. Purchas, III. 1880–1. Denys. (*Hist. nat. de l'Amerique Sept.* II, 387.)

[1] Purchas, III, 809. *Memoir of Sebastian Cabot*, pp. 108, 268, and the authorities there cited.

These facts not only prove that Newfoundland and Cape Breton were well known in France and Portugal before the Verrazzano voyage and therefore that he did not discover them, but that he must have known of them before, and that the letter is intentionally false in that respect. It might perhaps be insisted with some plausibility under other circumstances, that he ran along the coast, believing that it was a new land, and therefore made the representation of having discovered it in good faith. But admitting that it was even possible for him to have sailed along those shores without encountering a single fishing craft which would have assured him that he was not in unknown waters, it is impossible that he could have sailed from Dieppe and returned to that port where, of all the places in France or Europe, the knowledge of these facts most existed, and where they were as familiar as household words, and where they must have entered into the thoughts and hopes of many of its inhabitants, without their being known to him; and that he could have written the letter from that same port, claiming the discovery of the country for himself, without intending a fraud. It was the port to which Aubert belonged and where he landed the Indians he brought from Newfoundland. It was the principal port of Normandy from which the fishing vessels made their annual voyages to that country. It was the port from whence he manned and equipped his own fleet of four ships, with crews which must have been largely composed of Normand sailors who were familiar with the navigation and the coast. And there was not a citizen of Dieppe, probably, who had not an interest of some nature in one or more of the fishing vessels, and could have told him what country it was that he had explored.

It bears unequivocal testimony to the fictitious character of this claim, that Ramusio thought it necessary to interpolate in his version a passage representing the discovery of Verrazzano as terminating where the discoveries of the Bretons began, and to omit the cosmography which states it was at the point where those of the Portuguese towards the Arctic circle commenced. By this alteration the letter is made to acknowledge the prior discoveries by the Bretons, which are entirely excluded in the original version, and to adopt the latitude of 50° N. for the Verrazzano limit thus making the false statement, as to the extent of the discovery, a mistake as it were of nautical observation. The following parallel passages in two versions will best explain the character and effect of the alteration.

VERSION OF CARLI,
Narrative.

Navicando infra 'l subsolano ed aquilone in spatio di leghe CL e de già avendo consumato tutte le nostre substantie navale e vettovaglie, avendo discopruto leghe DII cive leghe 700, più di nuova terra fornendoci di acque et legue deliberammo di tornare in Francia.

* * * * * *

Cosmography.
In questa nostra navigatione fatta per ordine di V. S. M., oltre i gradi 92 che dal detto

VERSION OF RAMUSIO,
Narrative.

Navigando fra levante & tramontana per spatio di leghe 150, *pervenimo propinqui alla terra che per il passato trovorono i Brettoni, quale sta in gradi* 50 & havēdo horamai consumati tutti li nostri armeggi & vettovaglie, havendo scoperto leghe 700, & piu di nuova terra, fortinoci di acque & legue, deliberammo tornare in Francia.

* * * * * *

Cosmography omitted.

meridiano verso lo occidente della prima terra trovamo gradi 34 navigando leghe 300 infra oriente e settentrione leghe 400, quasi allo oriente continuo el lito della terra siamo pervenuti per infino a gradi 50, lasciando la terra che più tempo fa trovorno li Lusitani, quali seguirno più al septentrione, pervenendo sino al circulo artico e 'l fine lasciendo incognito.

Translation Narrative.

After sailing between east and north the distance of one hundred and fifty leagues more and finding our provisions and naval stores nearly exhausted, we took in wood and water, and determined to return to France having discovered VII that is 700 leagues of unknown lands.

*　*　*　*　*　*

Translation Narrative.

Sayling northeast for the space of 150 leagues *we approached to the lande that in times past was discovered by the Britons, which is in fiftie degrees.* Having now spent all our provision and victuals and having discovered about 700 leagues and more of newe countries, and being furnished with water and wood we concluded to returne into Fraunce.

(Hakluyt. *Divers voyages.*)

*　*　*　*　*　*

Cosmography.

In the voyage which we made by order of your Majesty, in addition to the 92 degrees we ran towards the west from our point of departure, before we reached land in the latitude of 34, we have to count 300 leagues which we ran northeastwardly, and 400 nearly east along the coast before *we reached the* 50*th parallel of north latitude, the point where we turned our course from the shore towards home. Beyond this point the Portuguese had already sailed* *as far north as the Arctic circle, without coming to the termination of the land.*

(Cogswell. *Coll. of N. Y. Hist. Society*, Second series, I.)

Ramusio in omitting the cosmography and confining his version to the narrative would have left the letter without any designation of the northerly limit reached by Verrazzano, had he not transferred to the narrative, the statement of the latitude attained, namely, the fiftieth degree, from the cosmographical part; which was therefore properly done, though as an editor he should have stated the fact. But he transcended his duty entirely in asserting, in qualification of the latitude, what does not appear in the letter, that it was near where the Bretons had formerly made discoveries, and omitting all reference to the Portuguese. The Bretons are not mentioned or even alluded to in either portion of the original letter. The effect of this substitution therefore is to relieve the original from making a false claim to the discovery north of Cape Breton, by admitting the discoveries of the Bretons, and making the alleged extent of the Verrazzano discovery, as already remarked, a mistake of nautical observation only. That it was deliberately made, and for that purpose, is shown by his taking the designation of the latitude from the same sentence in the cosmography as that in which the mention of the Portuguese discoveries occurs, in qualification of the latitude.

The motive which led Ramusio to make this alteration is found in the discourse of the French captain of Dieppe, in which it is stated that this part of the coast was discovered by the Normands and Bretons and the Portuguese, many years before the Verrazzano voyage. Ramusio, as he informs us himself, translated that paper from the French into the Italian and published it in the same volume, in conjunction with the Verrazzano letter, which he remodelled. He thus had the contents of both documents before him, at the same time, and saw the contradiction between them. They could not both be true. To reconcile them, alterations were necessary; and this change was made in the letter in order to make it conform to the discourse. The fact of his making it, proves that he regarded the letter as advancing an indefensible claim.

It is also to be observed that in adopting the fiftieth parallel as the extent of the discovery in the north, Ramusio obtained the statement from the cosmography, showing that he had that portion of the letter before him; and confirming the conclusion, expressed in a previous section, that his version was composed from the Carli copy of the letter, in which alone the cosmography occurs. Whether this limit was so transposed by him for a purpose or not, may be a question; but the origin of it cannot be disputed.

VI.

IV. THE DESCRIPTION OF THE PEOPLE AND PRODUCTIONS OF THE LAND NOT MADE FROM THE PERSONAL OBSERVATION OF THE WRITER OF THE LETTER. WHAT DISTINCTIVELY BELONGED TO THE NATIVES IS UNNOTICED, AND WHAT IS ORIGINALLY MENTIONED OF THEM IS UNTRUE. FURTHER IMPORTANT ALTERATIONS OF THE TEXT BY RAMUSIO.

We are brought now to the observations in reference to the people and productions of the country. The communications which the explorers had with the shore are not represented as having been numerous, or their visits of long duration, the longest having been one of three days, while they were riding at anchor off the coast of North Carolina, and another of fifteen, spent in replenishing the supplies for their ship, in the harbor in the great bay of Massachusetts. These opportunities were however, it seems, sufficient to have enabled them to study the characteristics of the natives and to determine the nature of the vegetation at those places; but the description given of both is very general. Not a single person, sagamore or warrior, or even the boy who was carried away to France, is designated by name, nor any object peculiar to the region by its native appellation. Not an Indian word, by which a locality or a tribe might be traced, occurs in the whole narrative. Some familiar details are mentioned of Indian manners and customs, which give the account the appearance of truth, but there is nothing in them which may not have been deduced from known narratives of earlier voyages to adjoining parts of America; while much that was peculiar to the country claimed to have been discovered, and of a character to compel observation, is omitted; and some particulars stated which could not have existed.

In its incidents of Indian life it recalls the experiences of Columbus. When the great discoverer first came to the island of Hispaniola it is related, "they saw certaine men of the Islande who perceiving an unknowen native comming toward them, flocked together and ran into the thicke woodes, as it had bin hares coursed with greyhoundes. Our men pursuing them took only one woman, whom they brought to the ships, where filling her with meate and wine, and apparrelling her, they let her depart to her companie." Also, "their boates are made only of one tree made hollow with a certain sharpe stone, for they have no yron, and are very long and narrow." And again, "when our men went to prayer, and kneeled on their knees, after the manner of the Christians, they did the like also. And after what manner soever they saw them pray to the crosse, they followed them in all poyntes as well as they could."[1] The Verrazzano letter tells us, in like phrase, that when they landed at the end of fifty leagues from the landfall, "we found that the people had fled to the woods for fear. By searching around we discovered in the grass a very old woman and a young girl of about eighteen or twenty, who had concealed themselves for the same reason. We gave them a

---

[1] Peter Martyr, Dec. I.I. in Eden.

ARTIFICIAL DESCRIPTION OF THE COUNTRY. 71

part of our provisions, which they accepted with delight, but the girl would not touch any." At the same place, it is added, " we saw many of their boats made of one tree, without the aid of stone or iron or other kind of metal." And to make the parallel complete, the letter asserts of the natives, "they are very easy to be persuaded and imitated us with earnestness and fervor in all which they saw us do as Christians in our acts of worship." While they were taking in their supplies and interchanging civilities with the Indians in the harbor of the great bay, the following scene of royalty is described as having occurred. " One of the two kings often came with his queen and many gentlemen (*gentili uomini*) to see us for his amusement, but he always stopped at the distance of about two hundred paces, and sent a boat to inform us of his intended visit, saying they would come and see our ship. This was done for safety, and as soon as they had an answer from us, they came off and remained awhile to look around; but on hearing the annoying cries of the sailors, the king sent the queen with her maids (*demizelle*) in a very light boat to wait near an island, a quarter of a league distant from us while he remained a long time on board." This hyperbolical description of the visit of the sachem of Cape Cod accompanied by the gentlemen of his household and of his squaw queen with her maids of honor, has its prototype in the visit paid to Bartholomew Columbus, during the absence of his brother, the admiral, by Bechechio the king or cacique of Xaragua and his sister, the queen dowager, Anacoana, who are represented as going to the ship of the Adelantado in two canoes, "one for himself and certayne of his gentlemen, another for Anacoana and her waiting women." The astonishment which the natives manifested at the appearance of the Dauphiny and her crew; their admiration of the simple toys and little bells which were offered them by the strangers; their practice of painting their bodies, adorning themselves with the gay plumage of birds, and habiting themselves with the skins of animals, seem all analogized, in the same way, from the accounts given by Peter Martyr of the inhabitants of the islands discovered by Columbus, and of the northern regions by Sebastian Cabot. These traits of Indian life and character, therefore, not having been peculiar to the natives of the country described in the letter, and having been already mentioned in earlier accounts of the adjoining parts of America, the description of them here furnishes no proof of originality or of the truth of the letter for that reason.

On the other hand objects which historically belong to the inhabitants of the places declared to have been visited, and characterize them distinctly from those previously discovered, and which were of such a marked character as to have commanded attention, are not mentioned at all. Of this class perhaps the most prominent is the wampum, a commodity of such value and use among them that, like gold among the Europeans, it served the double purpose of money and personal adornment. The region of the harbor where the voyagers spent, according to the letter, fifteen days in familiar intercourse with the inhabitants, was its greatest mart, from which it was spread among the tribes, both north and east. Wood, describing the Narragansets in 1634, says they "are the most curious minters of the wampompeage and mowhakes which they forme out of the inmost wreaths of periwinkle shels. The northerne, easterne, and westerne Indians fetch all their coyne from these southern mint-masters. From hence they have most of their curious pendants and bracelets; hence they have their great stone pipes which will hold a quarter of an ounce of tobacco." And in regard to their practice of ornamentation, he remarks again : " although they be poore, yet is there in them the sparkes of naturall pride which appeares in their longing desire after many kinde of ornaments, wearing pendants in their eares, as formes of birds, beasts and fishes, carved out of bone, shels, and stone, with long bracelets of their curious wrought wampompeage and mowhackees which they put about their necks and loynes; which they count a rare kinde of decking." The same writer adds a description of an Indian king of this country in his attire, which is somewhat less fanciful than that in the letter. " A sagamore with a humberd (humming-bird) in his eare for a pendant, a blackhawke in his occiput for his plume, mowhackees for his gold chaine, good store of wampompeage begirting his loynes, his bow in his hand, his quiver at his back, with six naked Indian spatterlashes at his heeles for his guard, thinkes himselfe little inferiour to the great Cham." [1] Roger Williams confirms this account of the importance of the wampum among these same Indians. "They hang," he states " these strings of money about their

---

[1] *New England Prospect*, pp. 61, 35-6.

necks and wrists, as also about the necks and wrists of their wives and children. Machequoce, a girdle, which they make curiously of one, two, three, four and five inches thickness and more, of this money, which sometimes to the value of tenpounds and more, they weare about their middle, and a scarfe about their shoulders and breasts.

> The Indians prize not English gold,
> Nor English, Indians shell :
> Each in his place will passe for ought,
> What ere men buy or sell." [1]

Another important article in universal use among the Indians of the main land, north and south, was the tobacco pipe. Tobacco was used by the natives of the West India islands, made up in rolls or cigars; but by the Indians of the continent it was broken up, carried in small bags attached to a girdle round the body, and smoked through clay, stone or copper pipes, sometimes of very elaborate workmanship. Smoking the pipe was of universal use among them, both on ordinary and extraordinary occasions. It was a tender of hospitality to strangers; and a sign of peace and friendship between the nations.[2] When Captain Waymouth ran along the coast of the great bay of Massachusetts, in 1605, he repeatedly encountered this custom. On one occasion the natives came from the shore in three canoes, and Rosier remarks of them : " they came directly aboord us and brought us tobacco, which we tooke with them *in their pipe* which was

---

[1] *Key into the Language of America*, pp. 149–50.

[2] For a full and interesting account of the importance of the tobacco-pipe among the Indians of North America, upon cited authorities, we refer the reader to *Antiquities of the Southern Indians*. By Charles C. Jones Jr., p. 382. (New York, 1873.)

ARTIFICIAL DESCRIPTION OF THE COUNTRY.   75

...de of earth very strong, but blacke and short, con-
...ining a great quantity. When we came at shoare
...ey all most kindely entertained us, taking us by the
...nds, as they had observed we did to them aboord in
...ken of welcome, and brought us to sit downe by their
...e, where sat together thirteene of them. They
...led their tobacco pipe, which was then the short
...aw of a lobster, which will hold ten of our pipes full
...d we dranke of their excellent tobacco, as much as
...e would with them."[1] No notice is taken of this
...istom, either of tobacco or the pipe in the Verrazzano
...tter.

The most remarkable omission of all is of the bark
...noe. This light and beautiful fabric was peculiar
...the Algonkin tribes. It was not found among the
...uthern Indians, much less in the West India islands.
...ts buoyancy and the beauty of its form were such
...s to render it an object of particular observation.
...hough so light as to be capable of being borne on a
...an's shoulders, it would sometimes carry nine men,
...nd ride with safety over the most stormy sea. It
...vas always from the first a great object of interest
...vith the discoverers of the northerly parts of the
...oast, which they manifested by taking them back to
...lurope, as curiosities. Aubert carried one of them to
...Dieppe in 1508, and Captain Martin Pringe, who was
...ne of the first to visit the shores of Cape Cod, took
...ne, in 1603, thence to Bristol, which he thus de-
...cribes, as if he saw no other kind.

"Their boats whereof we brought one to Bristoll, were in propor-
ion like a wherrie of the river of Thames, seventeene foot long and

---

[1] Purchas, IV. 1662.

foure foot broad, made of the barke of a birch tree, farre exceeding in bignesse those of England: it was sowed together with strong and tough oziers or twigs, and the seames covered over with rozen or turpentine little inferiour in sweetnesse to frankincense, as we made triall by burning a little thereof on the coales at sundry times after our comming home: it was also open like a wherrie, and sharpe at both ends, saving that the beake was a little bending roundly upward. And though it carried nine men standing upright, yet it weighed not at the most, above sixtie pounds in weight, a thing almost incredible in regard of the largeness and capacitie thereof. Their oares were flat at the end like an oven peele, made of ash or maple, very light and strong, about two yards long wherewith they row very swiftly."[1]

The silence of the letter in regard to this species of the canoe is the more remarkable, as it is in connection with the natives of the harbor where they spent fifteen days, that mention is made in it a second time of the manner of making their boats out of single logs, as if it were a subject of importance, and worthy of remark. The inference is most strongly to be drawn therefore, from this circumstance, that the writer knew nothing about the bark canoe, or the people who used them.

The absence of all allusion to any of the peculiar attributes, especially of the essential character just described, of the natives of the great bay leads to the conclusion that the whole account is a fabrication. But this end is absolutely reached by the positive statement of a radical difference in complexion between the tribes, which they found in the country.

The people whom they saw on their first landing, and who are stated to have been for the most part naked, are described as being black in color, and not very different from Ethiopians, (*di colore neri non*

---

[1] Purchas, IV. 1655.

ARTIFICIAL DESCRIPTION OF THE COUNTRY. 77

molto dagli Etiopi disformi) and of medium stature, well formed of body and acute of mind. The latter observation would imply that the voyagers had mixed with these natives very considerably in order to have been able to speak so positively in regard to their mental faculties, and therefore could not have been mistaken as to their complexion for want of opportunity to discover it. The precise place where they first landed and saw these black people is not mentioned further than that the country where they lived was situated in the thirty-fourth degree of latitude. From this place they proceeded further along the coast northwardly, and again coming to anchor attempted to go ashore in a boat without success, when one of them, a young sailor, attempted to swim to the land, but was thrown, by the violence of the waves, insensible on the beach. Upon recovering he found himself surrounded by natives who were black like the others. That there is no mistake in the design of the writer to represent these people as really black, like negroes, is made evident by his account of the complexion of those he found in the harbor of the great bay in latitude 41° 40', who are described as essentially different and the finest looking tribe they had seen, being " of a very white complexion, some inclining more to white, and others to a yellow color" (*di colore bianchissimo ; alcuni pendano più in bianchezza, altri in colore flavo*). The difference between the inhabitants of the two sections of country, in respect to color, is thus drawn in actual contrast.

This is unfounded in fact. No black aborigines have ever been found within the entire limits of North

America, except in California where some are said to exist. The Indians of the Atlantic coast were uniformly of a tawny or yellowish brown color, made more conspicuous by age and exposure and being almost white in infancy. The first voyagers and early European settlers universally concur in assigning them this complexion. Reference need here be to such testimony only as relates to the two parts of the country where the distinction is pretended to have existed. The earliest mention of the inhabitants of the more southerly portion is when the vessels of Ayllon and Matienzo carried off sixty of the Indians from the neighborhood of the Santee, called the Jordan, in 1521, and took them to St. Domingo. One of them went to Spain with Ayllon. They are described by Peter Martyr, from sight, as *semifuscos uti nostri sunt agricolae sole adusti aestivo*, half brown, like our husbandmen, burnt by the summer sun.[1] Barlowe, in his account of the first expedition of Raleigh, which entered Pamlico sound, within the region now under consideration, describes the Indians whom he found there as of a " colour yellowish."[2] Captain John Smith, speaking of those of the Chesapeake, remarks, that they " are of a color brown when they are of age, but they are born white."[3] On the other hand the natives of Massachusetts and Rhode Island in latitude 41° 40' are described by the first explorers of that region in substantially the same terms. Brereton, who accompanied Gosnold in his first voyage to the Elisabeth

---

[1] Dec. VII, 2.
[2] Hakluyt, III. 248.
[3] Smith, *Map of Virgina*, 1612, p. 19.

ARTIFICIAL DESCRIPTION OF THE COUNTRY. 79

islands and the main land opposite, in 1602, mentions the natives there, as being of a complexion or color much like a dark olive."[1] Martin Pringe who visited Martha's Vineyard the next year and constructed there a barricade where the "people of the country came sometimes, ten, twentie, fortie or three score, and at one time one hundred and twentie at once," says, "these people are inclined to a swart, tawnie or chesnut colour, not by nature but accidentally."[2] And Roger Williams, partaking of the same idea as Pringe, that the swarthy color was accidental, testifies, almost in the same language as Captain Smith, that the Narragansets and others within a region of two hundred miles of them, were "tawnie by the sunne and their annoyntings, yet they were born white."[3] Thus the authorities flatly contradict the statement of black Indians existing in North Carolina, and a difference of color between the people of the two sections claimed to have been visited in this voyage.

Of an equally absurd and preposterous character is the statement made in reference to the condition in which the plants and vegetation were found. The grape particularly is mentioned in a manner which proves, beyond question, that the writer could not have been in the country. The dates which are given for the exploration are positive; and are conclusive in this respect. The Dauphiny is represented as having left Madeira on the 17th of January, and arrived on the coast on the 7th of March, that is,

---

[1] Purchas, IV. 1652.
[2] Ibid, IV. 1655.
[3] Roger Williams's *Key*, 52.

the 17th of that month, new style.[1] They left the harbor of the great bay, where they had remained for fifteen days on the 6th of May, which makes their arrival there to have been on the 21st of April, or first of May, N. S. They were thus during the months of March and April, engaged in coasting from the landfall to the great bay in latitude 41° 40′, during which period the observations relating to the intermediate country, consequently, must have been made. They left the coast, finally, in latitude 50° N., for the purpose of returning to France, in time to reach there and have the letter written announcing their arrival at Dieppe on the 8th of July, and therefore it must have been some time in June, at the latest; so that very little if any portion of the summer season was passed upon the coast of America.

In describing the country which they reached at the end of the fifty leagues north of the landfall, that is, near the boundary between North Carolina and Virgina, where they discovered the old woman and girl concealed in the *grass* and found the land generally, " abounding in forests filled with various kinds of trees but not of such *fragrance*" as those where they first landed, the writer gives a particular description of the condition in which they found the vines and flowers.

" We saw," he says, " many vines there growing naturally, which run upon, and entwine about the trees, as they do in Lombardy, and which if the husbandmen were to have under a perfect system of cultivation, would without doubt produce the *best wines*, because tasting (*beendo*, literally, drinking or sucking) *the fruit many times*, we perceived it was sweet and pleasant, not different from ours.

---

[1] See *ante*, page 4, *note*.

ARTIFICIAL DESCRIPTION OF THE COUNTRY. 81

They are held in estimation by them because wherever they grow they remove the small trees around them in order that the fruit may be able to germinate. We found wild roses, violets, lilies and many species of plants and *odoriferous flowers*, different from ours.[1]

The flavor and vinous qualities of the grapes are thus particularly mentioned as having been proven several times by eating the ripe and luscious fruit, and in language peculiarly expressive of the fact. According to the dates before given, this must have occurred early in the month of April, as the scene is laid upon the coast of North Carolina. There is no native vine which ever flowers in this country, north of latitude thirty-four, before the month of May, and none that ripens its fruit before July, which is the month assigned by Lawson for the ripening of the summer fox grape in the swamps and moist lands of North Carolina,—the earliest of all the grapes in that region.[2] North of latitude 41° no grape matures until the latter part of August. As the explorers are made to have left the shores of Newfoundland for home in June, at farthest, they were at no time on any part of the coast, in season to have been able to see or taste the ripe or unripe fruit of the vine. The representation of the letter in this respect depending both upon the sight and the taste, must, like that of the contrasted appearance of the natives, be regarded as deliberately made;

---

[1] "Vedemmo in quella molte vite della natura prodotte, quali alzando si avvoltano agli alberi come nella Cisalpina Gallia costumano; le quali se dagli agricultori avessino el perfetto ordine di cultura, senza dubbio produrrebbono ottimi vini, perche più volte il frutto di quello beendo, veggiendo suave e dolce, non dal nostro differente sono da loro tenuti in extimatione; impero che per tutto dove nascono, levano gli arbusculi circustanti ad causa il frutto possa gierminare. Trovamo rose silvestre et vivuole, gigli et molte sorte di erbe e fiori odoriferi da nostri differenti."

[2] *New Voyage to Carolina*, p. 602.

and consequently, the two as establishing the falsity of the description in those particulars, and thus involving the integrity and truth of the whole.

The liberty which Ramusio took with these passages in his version of the letter, demands notice, and adds his testimony again to the absurdity of the account. He doubtless knew, from the numerous descriptions which had been published, of the uniformity of the physical characteristics of the American Indians; and he certainly knew of it as regarded the natives of this coast, as is proven by his publication of Oviedo's account of the voyage of Gomez, made there in 1525, in which they are described, in the same volume with the Verrazzano letter.[1] His own experience, as to the climate of Venice, taught him also that grapes could not have ripened in the latitude and at the time of year assigned for that purpose. He had therefore abundant reason to question the correctness of the letter in both particulars. As in the case of the representation of the extent of the discovery, before mentioned, he did not hesitate to make them conform more to the truth. He amended the original in regard to the complexion of the natives represented as those first seen, by inserting in place of the words, applied to them, of " black and not much different from Ethiopians," the phrase, " brownish and not much unlike the Saracens" (*berrettini*[2] *& non molto dalli Saracini differenti*) by which they are likened to those Arabs whose complexion, " yellow, bordering on brown," is

---

[1] Tom. III. fol. 52, (ed. 1556).

[2] *Berrettini* is derived from *beretta*, the Turkish fez, a red cap, designating also the scarlet cap of the cardinals in the church of Rome.

ARTIFICIAL DESCRIPTION OF THE COUNTRY.

of a similar cast;[1] and in regard to the grapes, by substituting instead of, " tasting the fruit many times we perceived it was sweet and pleasant," the passage, " having often seen the fruit thereof *dried*, which was sweet and pleasant," (*havēdo veduto piu volte il frutto di quelle secco, che era suaue & dolce,*) by which he apparently obviates the objection, but in fact only aggravates it, by asserting what has never yet been heard of, among the Indians of this coast, the preservation of the grape by drying or otherwise.

It is evident that whatever may have been the motives of Ramusio in making these repeated alterations of the statements in the letter, they not only show his own sense of their necessity, but they have had the effect to keep from the world the real character of this narrative in essential particulars, until its exposure now, by the production of the Carli version.

---

[1] Pritchard, *Natural History of Man*, p. 127 (2d edition).

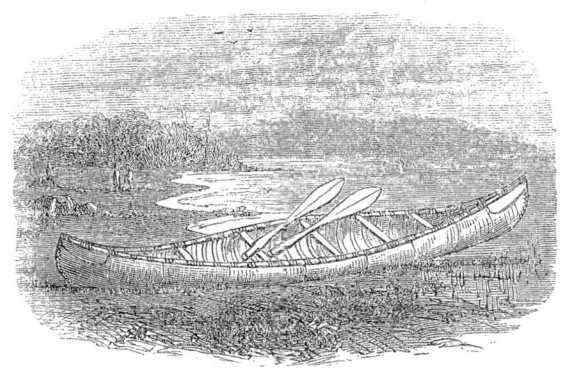

BIRCH BARK CANOE.
Still used by the Indians on the Penobscot.

VII.

THE EXTRINSIC EVIDENCE IN SUPPORT OF THE CLAIM. I. DISCOURSE OF THE FRENCH SEA-CAPTAIN OF DIEPPE.

The extrinsic evidence which is urged in support of the claim to the discovery by Verrazzano is not of great amount. It is certain, however, that if the letter upon which the claim is founded, be spurious and fictitious, as for the reasons assigned, it is considered to be, any extraneous evidence, must either partake of the same character, or have originated in some misconception or error. What exists upon the subject consists principally of two pieces, which have only recently been regarded of any importance for this purpose, and in connection with which the others may be considered.

One of them is an anonymous paper entitled in full, "Discourse of a great sea-captain, a Frenchman of the town of Dieppe, as to the voyages made to the new land of the West Indies, called New France, from the 40° to the 47° under the Arctic pole, and concerning the land of Brazil, Guinea, the island of St. Lawrence and that of Sumatra:" the other is a map of the world, bearing the name of Hieronimo de Verrazano.

The discourse of the French captain does not, any more than the letter of Verrazzano, exist in the original; nor has any copy of it ever been produced, except in a printed translation by Ramusio in the same volume, as that in which his version of that letter appears, and immediately following it. Ramusio states that it was written in 1539, as may be inferred from the letter itself in its present form, and that he had translated it from the French, grieving much that he did not know the name of the author, because not giving it he seemed to do wrong to the memory of so valiant and noble a gentleman. It is evident, however, upon comparing the description, which it gives, of a voyage made from Dieppe to Sumatra, with the original journal, first brought to light and published a few years ago, of such a voyage made by Jean Parmentier in 1529, that this discourse was written by some one of the persons engaged in that expedition.[1] Its authenticity, in general, may therefore not be questioned. But as the original has never been produced and it is only known through this version of Ramusio, experience in regard to his practice as a compiler, of altering texts according to his judgment of their defects and errors, proves that we have by no means a reliable copy for our guidance. In fact, as given by Ramusio, its recognition of the Verrazzano discovery is only by way of parenthesis, and in such antagonism to the context, as to render it quite certain that this portion of it is by another hand.

---

[1] *Voyages et découvertes des navigateurs Normands.* Par L. Estancelin, p. 241. (Paris 1832.) M. Estancelin supposes that Pierre Mauclere the astronomer of one of the ships composing the expedition of Parmentier, was the author of this discourse (p. 45 *note*). But M. D'Avezac attributes it to Pierre Crignon, who also accompanied Parmentier, and who besides being the editor of a collection of poems by Parmentier, after his death, evinced his knowledge of nautical matters by writing a dissertation on the variation of the needle. *Introduction* to the *Brief Recit* of Jacques Cartier, p. VII. (Tross, Paris, 1863.) Brunet, *sub* Parmentier. Margry, *Les navigateurs Françaises*, p. 199.

The writer, after explaining the nature of latitude and longitude, and taking the meridian of no variation running through the eastern extremity of the Cape de Verde islands as the basis of his observations of longitude, proceeds to a description of Terra Nova; so much of which as is pertinent is here abstracted.

"The Terra Nova, the nearest cape of which is called the Cape de Ras, is situated west of our diametrical or meridional line whereon is fixed the first point of longitude according to the true meridian of the compass; and the said Cape de Ras is in west longitude 40° and 47 of North latitude. The Terra Nova extends towards the Arctic pole from 40° to 60, and from Cape de Ras going towards the pole, the coast almost always runs from south to north, and contains in all 350 leagues, and from said Cape de Ras to the cape of the Brettons, the coast runs east and west, for an hundred leagues, and the cape of the Brettons is in 47° west longitude and 46 north latitude. To go from Dieppe to the Terra Nova, the course is almost all east and west, and there are from Dieppe to said Cape de Ras 760 leagues.

"Between Cape de Ras and cape of the Brettons dwell an austere and cruel people with whom you cannot treat or converse. They are large of person, clad in skins of seals and other wild animals tied together, and are marked with certain lines, made with fire, on the face and as it were striped with color between black and red, (*tra il nero & berrettino*) and in many respects as to face and neck, are like those of our Barbary, the hair long like women, which they gather up on top of the head as we do with a horse's tail. Their arrows are bows with which they shoot very dexterously, and their arrows are pointed with black stones and fish bones. * * * *

"This land was discovered 35 years ago, that is, the part that runs east and west, by the Brettons and Normands, for which reason the land is called the Cape of the Brettons. The other part that runs north and south was discovered by the Portuguese from Cape de Ras to Cape Buona-vista, which contains about 70 leagues, and the rest was discovered as far as the gulf of the Castles, and further on by said Brettons and Normands, and it is about 33 years since a ship from Honfleur of which Jean Denys (Giovanni Dionisio) was captain and Camart (Camarto) of Rouen, was pilot, first went there, and in the year 1508, a Dieppe vessel, called the Pensee, which was owned by Jean Ango, father of Monsignor, the captain and Viscount of

Dieppe went thither, the master or the captain of said ship being Thomas Aubert, and he was the first who brought hither people of the said country.

"Following beyond the cape of the Brettons there is a land contiguous to the said cape, the coast whereof extends west by southwest as far as the land of Florida and it runs full 500 leagues, (*which coast was discovered fifteen years ago, by Messer Giovanni da Verrazzano, in the name of King Francis, and Madame the regent,*) and this land is called by many la Francese, and likewise by the Portuguese themselves and its end towards Florida is at 78° west longitude and 30° north latitude. The inhabitants of this land are tractable peoples, friendly and pleasant. The land is most abundant in all fruit. There grow oranges, almonds, wild grapes and many other kinds of odoriferous trees. The land is called by its people Nurumbega, and between this land and that of Brazil is a great gulf which extends westwardly to 92° west longitude, which is more than a quarter of the circuit of the globe; and in the gulf are the islands and West Indies discovered by the Spaniards." [1]

This account emphatically contradicts the Verrazzano letter which claims the discovery of the coast from Cape Breton in 46° N. as far east and north as 50° N. latitude, embracing a distance of two hundred leagues, both according to the letter and the discourse. It distinctly affirms this long stretch of coast to have been discovered long before the Verrazzano voyage by the Portuguese and the Bretons and Normands, assigning to the Portuguese and French specific portions of it. This is in perfect harmony with the truth as established by the authorities to which occasion has already been had to refer. This account therefore unequivocally repudiates the Verrazzano claim to the discovery of that part of the country, and thus derogates from the pretensions of the letter instead of supporting them.

The letter contains a distinct and specific claim for the discovery of the coast as far north as 50° N. The

---

[1] Ramusio, III. fol. 423-4 (ed. 1556).

writer of the discourse, if he had any knowledge on the subject, must have known of the extent of this claim. In attributing to others the discovery of that large portion of the coast, east and north of Cape Breton, he must have considered the claim to that extent as unfounded. It is difficult therefore to account for his admitting its validity as regards the country south of Cape Breton as he apparently does; as it is a manifest inconsistency to reject so important a part as false, and affirm the rest of it to be true, when the whole depends upon the same evidence.

Another circumstance to be remarked is, that the description, which follows, of the country said to have been discovered by Verrazzano, has not the slightest reference to the account given in the letter, but is evidently derived from other sources of discovery. Two names are attributed to it, *Francese* and *Nurumbega*, both of which owe their designation to other voyagers. Francese, or French land, appears for the first time in any publication, on two maps hereafter mentioned, printed in 1540, under the Latin form of Francisca. It is called in the manuscript cosmography and charts of Jean Alfonse, *terre de la Franciscane*. An earlier map by Baptista Agnese, described by Mr. Kohl, indicates that the name owes its origin, as will hereafter be pointed out, to the voyages of the French fishermen to the shores of Nova Scotia and New England.[1] Nurumbega, as the writer himself states, is an Indian name, which could not have been taken from the Verrazzano account, as that does not mention a single Indian word of any kind. The statement of the productions

---

[1] *Discovery of Maine*, p. 202, chart XIV.

of the country includes oranges, which do not belong to any portion of the continent claimed to have been visited by Verrazzano, and plainly indicates an entirely different authority for that portion of the coast. It is therefore equally unaccountable why the author of the discourse should have acknowledged the discovery by Verrazzano and, at the same time, have passed over altogether the description in the letter, and sought his information in regard to the country elsewhere, when he had there such ample details, especially in connection with the great bay.

The solution of the whole difficulty is to be found in the fact that the clause relating to Verrazzano was not the work of the author of the discourse, but of another person. It is not difficult to understand how and by whom this interpolation came to be made. Ramusio had both the letter and the discourse in his hands at the same time, for the purpose of preparing them for publication, recomposing the one, as has already been shown, and translating the other from the French into the Italian, as he himself states. In the execution of the former of these tasks, he took the liberty of altering the letter, as has been proven, by substituting the phrase of, *the land discovered by the Bretons*, for that of, *the country explored by the Portuguese*, as the northern limit of the voyage of Verrazzano; thereby removing the objection, to which the letter was obnoxious, of entirely ignoring the discoveries of the Bretons, which were distinctly asserted in the discourse. In order to conform to the Verrazzano letter, as it was thus modified, it was necessary to insert this clause in the discourse, which would else appear to contradict the letter entirely. The two alterations, however necessary they were to preserve some consistency between the two documents, are, nevertheless, both alike repugnant to the original letter.

This discourse fails, therefore, as an authority in favor of the Verrazzano discovery, or even of the existence of a claim in its behalf; the statement which it contains in relation to Verrazzano, originating with Ramusio adding nothing to the case.[1]

---

[1] The writer gives, however, some details in relation to the Indians and the fisheries along the easterly coast of Newfoundland, illustrative of certain points which have arisen in the course of this enquiry. Continuing his remarks, as given in the text, in regard to the Indians inhabiting the southerly coast between Cape Race and Cape Breton, he states: " there are many stags and deer, and birds like geese and *margaux*. On the coast there is much good fishery of cod, which fish are taken by the *French and Bretons, only because those of the country do not take them*. In the coast running north and south, from Cape de Ras to the entrance of the Castles, [straits of Belle-Isle] there are great gulfs and rivers, and numerous islands, many of them large; and this country is thinly inhabited, except the aforesaid coast, and the people are smaller; and there is great fishery of cod as on the other coast. There has not been seen there either village, or town, or castle, except a great enclosure of wood, which was seen in the gulf of the Castles; and the aforesaid people dwell in little cabins and huts, covered with the bark of trees, which they make to live in during the time of the fisheries, which commences in spring and lasts all the summer. Their fishery is of seal, and porpoises which, with certain seafowl called margaux, they take in the islands and dry; and of the grease of said fish they make oil, and when the time of their fishery is ended, winter coming on, they depart with their fish, and go away, *in little boats made of the bark of trees*, called *buil*, into other countries, which are perhaps warmer, but we know not where."

VIII.

II. The Verrazano Map. It is not an Authoritative Exposition of the Verrazzano Discovery. Its Origin and Date in its Present Form. The Letter of Annibal Caro. The Map presented to Henry VIII. Voyages of Verrazzano. The Globe of Euphrosynus Ulpius.

The map of Hieronimo de Verrazano, recently brought to particular notice,[1] is a planisphere on a roll of parchment eight feet and a half long and of corresponding width, formerly belonging to Cardinal Stefano Borgia, in whose museum, in the college of the Propaganda in the Vatican, it is now preserved. It has no date, though, from a legend upon it referring to the Verrazzano discovery, it may be inferred that the year 1529 is intended to be understood as the time when it was constructed. No paleographical description of it, however, has yet been published, from which the period of its construction might be determined, or the congruity of its parts verified. It may, however, in order to disencumber the question, be admitted to be the map mentioned by Annibal Caro in 1537, in a letter to which occasion will hereafter be had to refer, and that its author was the brother of the navigator, though of both these facts satisfactory proof is wanting.[2]

---

[1] *Journal of the American Geographical Society of New York.* 1873 Vol. IV. *Notes on the Verrazano map.* By James Carson Brevoort.

[2] This map was either unknown to Ramusio and Gastaldi or discredited by them. Ramusio in his preface, after mentioning to Fracastor that he

92   VERRAZZANO.

No entirely legible copy of this map has yet been made public. Two photographs, both much reduced from the original, have been made for the American Geographical Society, from the larger of which, so much as relates to the present purpose, has been carefully reproduced here on the same scale. It is to be regretted that the names along the coast, and the legends relating to the Verrazzano exploration, are not photographed distinctly, though the legends and a few names have been supplied by means of a pen. But although a knowledge of all the names is necessary for a thorough understanding of this map, these photographs, nevertheless, affording a true transcript of it in other respects, enable us to determine that it is of no authority as to the alleged discovery itself.[1]

It will be found, in the first place, to contravene the Verrazzano letter as to the limits of the discovery, both north and south, and to indicate merely an attempt to reconcile that discovery generally with the

---

placed the relation of Verrazzano and Jacques Cartier in that volume, adds, that inasmuch as Fracastor had exhorted him to make, in imitation of Ptolemy, four or five maps of as much as was known up to that time of the part of the world recently discovered, he could not disobey his commands, and had therefore arranged to have them made by the Piedmontese cosmographer, Giacomo de Gastaldi. They are accordingly to be found in the same volume with the letter of Verrazzano. One of them is a map of New France extending somewhat south of Norumbèga, but no features of the Verrazano map are to be traced upon it: and no other map of the country is given. Fol. 424–5.

[1] This map was first brought to public notice by M. Thomassey, in a memoir entitled, *Les Papes Géographes et la Cosmographie du Vatican*, which was published in the *Nouvelles Annales des Voyages*. Nouvelle serie, tome xxxv. Annee 1853. Tome Troisieme. Paris. We are indebted to this memoir for the explanation on our copy of the map of the scale of distances, which is illegible on the photographs. According to this explanation there should be nine points in the narrower, and nineteen in the wider spaces. These being two and a half leagues apart, give twenty-five leagues for the smaller and fifty leagues for the larger spaces, making three hundred and fifty leagues for the whole scale.

discoveries of the Spaniards, Bretons and Portuguese, as shown on the maps of the period to which it relates.

The coast of North America is laid down continuously from the gulf of Mexico to Davis straits, in latitude 60° N. Beginning at the point of Florida, which is placed *in latitude* 33½° *N.*, more than eight degrees north of its true position, it runs northerly along the Atlantic, trending slightly to the west, to a bay or river, in latitude 38° N. On this part of the country, called Terra Florida, the arms of Spain are represented, denoting its discovery by the Spaniards : and the whole of its coast for a distance of eighty or ninety leagues, is entirely devoid of names.

From 38° N. that is, from the land of Florida as here shown, the coast continues in a northerly direction thirty or forty leagues further, to a point between 40° and 41° N. when, turning northeasterly, it runs with slight variations, on a general course of east north east, for six hundred and fifty leagues to Cape Breton placed in latitude 51½ N., five and a half degrees north of it true position. Along this part of the coast more than sixty names of places occur at intervals sufficiently regular to denote one continuous exploration. They are for the most part undistinguishable on the photographs, but nine of them, at the beginning, are made legible by hand, the first two of which commencing *at latitude* 38°, are *Dieppa* and *Livorno*. The others, proceeding north, are *Punta de Calami, Palamsina, Pdara flor, Comana, Santiago, C. d' Olimpe*, and *Olimpe*, indicating a nomenclature different from that used on any other known map of this region. At a distance of three hundred leagues from Dieppa, and *in latitude* 46° *N.*, is a large triangular island, designated by the name of *Luisia*. Hence to Cape Breton the names are illegibly photographed. Along this coast, at three points, namely, in latitude 42°; opposite the island of Luisia, in latitude 46; and in latitude 50°, standards are displayed, the nationality of which cannot be distinguished, but which no doubt were intended for those of France, inasmuch as over them occurs the name of *Nova Gallia sive Iucatanet* in large, commanding letters, with the Verrazzano legend, before referred to underneath it, in these words: '*Verrazana seu Gallia nova quale discopri 5 anni fa Giovanni di Verrazano fiorentino per ordine et comandamēte del Chrystianissimo Re di Francia;* that is, Verrazzana or New Gaul which Giovanni di Verrazzano, a Florentine, discovered *five years ago* by order and command of the most Christian king of France.[1]

Over Cape Breton is a representation of the shield of Brittany, denoted by its ermines, in token of the discovery of that country by the Bretons, which is separated by a bay or gulf from *Terra Nova sive Le Molue*, the latter term being evidently intended for Bacalao (codfish, *Fr.* morue), the received name of Newfoundland. The southerly coast of Terra Nova for an hundred leagues, and its easterly coast running to the north, are delineated, with the Portuguese name of *C. Raso* and the island of *Baccalaos* barely legible. The coast runs north from C. Raso to *C. Formoso* in latitude 60° where it meets the straits which separate it

---

[1] The names Verrazzana and Verrazzano in this legend are *written* on the photograph by hand, with a double z, though M. Thomassey uses only the single z, which is adopted on our copy. It would be a singular circumstance, leading to some speculation, if they should really be spelt with the two z's on the original. Hieronimo, if he were the brother of Giovanni, would hardly have written his own name, as it is inscribed on the map, with one z, and that of his brother with two, in the same document.

from *Terra Laboratoris*, the country discovered by Gaspar Cortereal on his first voyage, but here attributed to the English, and being in fact Greenland.[1]

It is obvious that the discoveries of Verrazzano are thus intended to embrace the coast from latitude 38° N. to Cape Breton, that is, between the points designated by the armorial designations of Spain and Brittany, and not beyond either, as that would make the map contradict itself. That they begin at the parallel 38 is shown by the names of Dieppa and Livorno, (Leghorn), which commemorate the port to which the expedition of Verrazzano belonged, and the country in which he himself was born. These names cannot be associated with any other alleged expedition. They are given on the map which contains the legend declaring the country generally to have been discovered by him; and are not found on any other. There can be no doubt, therefore, that they are meant to indicate the beginning of his exploration in the south.

That his discoveries are represented as extending in the north to Cape Breton is proven by the continuation of the names to that point, showing an exploration by some voyager along that entire coast, and by the absence of any designation of its discovery by any other nation than the French; while the distance from Dieppa to Cape Breton is laid down as seven hundred leagues, the same as claimed for this exploration.

But in restricting his discoveries to latitude 38° N.

---

[1] Mr. Brevoort gives other names as legible on the easterly coast of Terra Nova, which we have not been able to distinguish, namely: *c. de spera, illa de san luis, monte de rigo,* and *illa dos aves.* Mr. B. reads IUCATANET, and M. Margry YUCATANET, where our engraver has IUCATANIA, for the general name of the country. The word in either form is apochryphal, as *Yucatan* is designated in its proper place, though as an island; but which form is correct cannot be determined from the photograph.

on the south, this map essentially departs from the claim set up in the letter ascribed to Verrazzano which carries them to fifty leagues south of 34°; and on the other hand, in limiting them, in the north, to the land discovered by the Bretons, it conforms to its Portuguese authorities, upon which, as will be seen, it was founded, but, in so doing, contradicts the letter which extends them to the point where the Portuguese commenced their explorations to the Arctic circle, which this map itself shows were on the east side of Terra Nova. Verrazzano the navigator, therefore, could not have been the author of the letter and also the authority for the map.

That this map did not proceed from him is also proven by the representation upon it of a great ocean, called Mare Occidentale, which is laid down between the parallels within which these discoveries are confined. It lies on the west side of the continent but approaches so near the Atlantic, in latitude 41° N., that is, in the vicinity of New York, that according to a legend describing it, the two oceans are there only six miles apart, and can be seen from each other. This isthmus occurs several hundred miles north of Dieppa, and therefore at a point absolutely fixed within the limits of the Verrazzano discoveries, and where the navigator must have sailed, according to both the letter and the map, whether the latitudes on the map be correctly described or not. This western sea is thus made by its position a part of the discoveries of Verrazzano, and is declared by the legend to have been actually seen; and as he was the discoverer, it must be intended to have been seen by him. As, however, there is no such sea in reality, Verrazzano could never have seen it; and

THE VERRAZANO MAP.   97

therefore, he could not have so represented; or if he did, then the whole story must for that reason alone be discredited. There is no escape from this dilemma. Verrazzano could not have been deceived and have mistaken some other sheet of water for this great sea, and so represented it on any chart, or communicated it in any other way to the maker of this map; for he makes no mention of the circumstance in his letter to the king to whom he would have been prompt to report so important a fact; as it would have proved the accomplishment of the object of his voyage,— the discovery of a passage through this region to Cathay, or if not a passage, at least a way, which could have been made available for reaching the land of spices and aromatics, by reason of its low grade, evident by one sea being seen from the other, and its short distance.

The unauthentic character of this map, and the manner in which its representation of the Verrazzano discoveries was produced, distinctly appear in its method of construction. Cape Breton and Terra Nova are represented as they are laid down on the charts of Pedro Reinel and the anonymous cartographer,— reproduced on the first and fourth sheets of the Munich atlas and unquestionably belonging to the period anterior to the discovery of the continuity of the land from Florida to Cape Breton. They bear the names which are found on those maps, importing their discovery thus early by the Bretons and Portuguese. In the south, the designation of Florida as a Spanish discovery, with its southerly coast running along the parallel of thirty-three and a half of north latitude, eight degrees north of its actual position, is precisely the same as it is shown on the anonymous Portuguese chart just mentioned. These representations of the country, in the north and the south, were thus adopted as the basis of this map. But as there were not seven hundred leagues of coast between latitude 38° and Cape Breton, which is the distance it indicates as having been explored by Verrazzano, that extent could be obtained only, either by changing the latitude of Florida or Cape Breton, or prolonging the coast longitudinally, or both. The latitude of the northerly limit of Florida having been preserved for the commencement of the discoveries, Cape Breton had therefore to be changed and was accordingly carried five degrees and a half further north and placed in latitude $51\frac{1}{2}$ instead of 46, and by consequence the whole line of coast was thrown several degrees in that direction, as is proven by the position of the island of Louise, which thus falls in 46° N. instead of 41°, the latitude assigned to it in the letter. Nothing could more conclusively show the factitious origin of this delineation and its worthlessness as an exposition of the Verrazzano discovery.

Some importance, however, attaches to this map in its assisting us to fix approximately the time of the fabrication of the Verrazzano letter. If it were constructed in 1529, as some would infer, with the portions relating to the discovery upon it, then it is the earliest recognition of the *claim* to this discovery yet produced, irrespective of the letter. But it is by no means certain that it was originally made in that year. Nothing appears on the map itself giving that date in terms; but it is left to be inferred exclusively from the language of the legend, which states that the discovery was made *five years ago,* without any indication, either in the legend itself or elsewhere on the map, to what time that period relates; and leaving the discovery, therefore, to be ascertained from extraneous sources. If the discovery be assumed to have been made in 1524, then indeed the map, according to the legend, would have been constructed in 1529. But no person, unacquainted with the letter, can determine from this inscription, or any other part of the map, the date either of the discovery or map; and this precise difficulty Euphrosynus Ulpius apparently encountered in attempting to fix the time of the discovery for his globe, as will hereafter be seen. Why the time of the discovery should have been left in such an ambiguous state, compatibly with fair intentions, it is difficult to understand. The year itself could and should, in the absence of any date on the map, have been stated directly in the legend, without compelling a resort to other authorities. It is not unusual, it is true, for valuable maps and charts of this period to be left without the dates of their construction upon them; but when, as in this case, a date is called for, there seems to be no reason why it should not have been given. This circumstance creates the suspicion that the legend did not belong to the map originally, but was added afterwards, as it now appears on the copy in the Vatican; or if it were upon it then, that it was intended to mislead and conceal the true date of the map. But whatever may be the secret of its origin, this legend furnishes no positive evidence as to the time when the map was made, or pretended to have been made; and we are left to find its date, if possible, by other means.

A fact which indicates that this map could not have existed as late as 1536, in the form in which it is now presented, if it existed then at all, is that the western sea is delineated upon a map of the world, made in that year, by Baptista Agnese, an Italian cosmographer, without any reference to the Verrazzano discoveries, under circumstances which would have led him to have recognized them if he knew of them, and which would have required him to have done so if this map were his authority. This sea is laid down by Agnese in the same manner as it is shown on the Verrazano map, approaching the Atlantic, from the north, along a narrow isthmus terminating at latitude 40°, with the coast turning abruptly to the west; the ocean being thus represented open thence from the isthmus to Cathay. A track of French navigation, not a single voyage, expressed by the words: *el viages de France*, is designated upon it, leading from the north of France to this isthmus, referring obviously to the voyages of the fishermen of Brittany and Normandy, to the coasts of Nova Scotia and New England. No allusion is made to the voyage of Verrazzano, or to the discoveries attributed to him by the Verrazano map. The Atlantic coast on the contrary, is plainly delineated after the Spanish map of Ribero, as is shown by the form, peculiar to that map, of the coast, at latitude 40°, returning to the west. It is apparent, therefore, that the two maps of Agnese and Verrazano, both representing the western sea in the same form, must have been derived from a common source, or else one was taken from the other; and that the map of Agnese could not, in either case, have been derived from a map showing the Verrazzano discovery, and must consequently have been anterior to the Verrazano map in its present form.

It militates against the authenticity of the Verrazano map and the early date which it would have inferred for itself, that there is not a single known map or chart, either published or unpublished, before the great map of Mercator in 1569, that refers to the Verrazzano discoveries, or recognizes this map in any respect before that of Michael Lok, published by Hakluyt, in 1582; or any before Lok, that applies the name of the sea of Verrazano to the western sea. The unauthenticated and until recently unnoticed globe of Euphrosynus Ulpius, purporting to have been constructed in 1542, of which we will speak presently, is the only evidence yet presented of the existence of the Verrazano map, as it now appears, beyond the map itself. The whole theory of the early influence of the Verrazzano discovery, or of the Verrazano map, upon the cartography of the period to which they relate, and its consequently proving their authenticity, as advanced by some learned writers, is therefore incorrect and is founded in a misconception of fact.

This mistake relates to a map which is found in several editions of the geography of Ptolemy printed at Basle, supposed to represent the western sea shortly after the Verrazzano discovery, and consequently as derived from that source. Mr. Kohl,[1] in a chapter specially devoted to the consideration of charts from Verrazzano, reproduces one (No. xv. *a*) which he

---

[1] We are indebted entirely to Mr. Kohl for our knowledge of the map of Agnese, which he produces, on a reduced scale, in the *Discovery of Maine*, (chart xiv), with an account of the map and its author (p. 292).

describes as a sketch of North America, from a map of the new world, in an edition of Ptolemy printed in Basle, 1530. And he adds: "the map was drawn and engraved *a few years after Verrazano's expedition.* The plate upon which it was engraved, must have been in use for a long time; for the same map appears both in *earlier* and much later editions of Ptolemy. The same also reappears in the cosmography of Sebastian Münster, published in Basle." Mr. K. finally observes in regard to it: "this map has this particular interest for us, that it is probably the first on which the sea of Verrazano was depicted in the form given to it by Lok, in 1582. I have found no map *prior to* 1530, on which this delineation appears."[1] There is a little confusion of dates in this statement. Mr. K. states, however, that he had not seen the map of Hieronimo de Verrazano, and evidently derives his information, in regard to the sea of Verrazano, from the map of Lok, who alone gives the western sea the name of *Mare de Verrazana,* no doubt because he found the sea laid down on the map presented by Verrazzano to Henry VIII, to which reference will presently be made. Had Mr. K. seen the Verrazano map with the absurd legend upon it, in effect declaring the western sea to have been observed by Verrazzano, he must have arrived at different conclusions, notwithstanding the map in Ptolemy of the supposed early date. Mr. Brevoort, in his notes on the Verrazano map, probably relying on the authority of Mr. Kohl, says, " that the first published map containing traces of Verrazano's explorations, is in the Ptolemy of Basle, 1530, which appeared *four years before the*

---

[1] *Discovery of Maine,* pp. 296–7.

French renewed their attempts at American exploration. It shows the western sea without a name, and the land north of it is called Francisca." [1] The inference left to be drawn is that the presence of the French in this region, as denoted by the name, Francisca, four years before the discoveries in that quarter, by Jacques Cartier, and by the delineation of the western sea upon the Verrazano map, establish the authenticity both of the voyage of Verrazzano and the map.

All this is erroneous. There was no edition of Ptolemy published in 1530 at Basle, or elsewhere, known to bibliographers. The map to which reference is made, and which is reproduced by Mr. Kohl, was first printed in 1540 at Basle, in an edition of Ptolemy with new maps, both of the new and old world, and with new descriptions of the countries embraced in them, printed on the back of each, accompanied by a geographical description of the modern state of the countries of the old world by Sebastian Münster.[2] In all the editions of Ptolemy, containing maps of the new world, before the year 1540, North America was represented according to the mistaken ideas of Waltzemüller on that subject in 1513, and without regard to the discoveries which took place after his edition. The maps of Münster constituted a new departure of the Ptolemies in this respect, and were intended to represent the later discoveries in the new world. They were reprinted several times at Basle by the same printer,

---

[1] *Journal of Am. Geog. Soc. of New York*, vol. IV, p. 279.

[2] *Geographia Universalis, vetus et nova, complectens Claudii Ptolemæi Alexandrini enarrationis libros* VIII. * * * *Succedunt tabulæ Ptolemaicæ, opera Sebastiani Munsteri nouo parata modo. His adjectæ sunt plurime nouæ tabulæ, modernā orbis faciem literis & pictura explicantes, inter quas quædam antehac Ptolemæo non fuerunt additae.* Sm. fol. Basiteæ apud Henricum Petrum Mense Martio Anno MDXL.

Henri Pierre (Lelewell II. 176, 208). In the first edition, which is now lying before us, the map in question, number 45, bears the title of *Novæ Insalæ* XVII. *Nova Tabula*. It is an enlarged representation of the portion relating to the new world of another map, No. 1, in the same volume, called *Typus Universalis*, a map of the whole world, which appears here also as a new map, and represents, for the first time in the Ptolemaic series, the straits of Magellan in the south, New France in the north, and the coast running continuously, north and *northeast*, from Florida to Newfoundland.

Upon this map a deep gulf is shown, indenting America from a strait in the north, which leads from the Atlantic to the Pacific, in the region of Hudson's straits, in latitude 60° N. This gulf runs southerly into the continent as far as latitude 40° N., approaching the Atlantic coast, and in that respect, alone, conforms to the representation of the western sea on the maps of Verrazano and Lok. It differs materially, however, from that sea, and indicates an entirely different meaning and origin. It is simply a gulf, or deep bay, like Hudson's bay, but reaching further south, being landlocked on all sides, except the north, as high as latitude 60° N.; whereas the western sea, on the other maps, is, as already observed, an open sea, extending westerly from the isthmus in latitude 40°, without intervening land, uninterruptedly to India. The intention of the delineation of this portion of the map, is not equivocal. For the first time, on any map, there is found upon it the name of Francisca, which is placed above the parallel of 50° N. latitude and above that of *C. Britonum*, designated thus by name, in the proper position of Cape Breton. It is placed between the river St. Lawrence, which also is represented but not named, and the gulf before mentioned. This name, Francisca,[1] or the *French land,* and the position, indicate the then recent discoveries in that region, which were due to the French under Jacques Cartier, and which could properly belong to no other exploration of the French. The gulf, no doubt, relates to the great lakes or fresh water sea of which Cartier had heard from the natives, as he himself mentions. (Hakluyt, III. 225.)

With the correction, therefore, of the date of the Münster map, the argument in favor of the authenticity either of the Verrazzano discovery or of the Verrazano map, based upon the recognition by the Münster map, of that discovery immediately after it is alleged to have taken place, or after the alleged construction of the Verrazano map, in 1529, and before any other voyages were made by the French to that region, falls entirely to the ground. And with the actual representation upon it of the discoveries of Cartier, without any allusion to the alleged discoveries of Verrazzano or the pretensions of the Verrazano map, while giving the latest discoveries in America, it is fairly to be concluded that both were unheard of, or utterly discredited by the author of the Münster map.

The map of Agnese stands, therefore, as the earliest chart of an acknowledged date showing the western sea, and that is independently of the Verrazzano discovery, or the Verrazano map. The hitherto unpublished maps produced by Mr. Kohl, also for the purpose of proving the influence of the Verrazzano discovery, fail entirely of that object. The first of them,

---

[1] Called *Francese* in the discourse of the French captain of Dieppe.

in point of date, the sketch (No. xv. *c*) from the portolano of 1536, preserved in the Bodleian library at Oxford, shows a track of navigation from the north of France, across the Atlantic, *running between the Bacalaos and the land of the Bretons, through the gulf of St. Lawrence, to the Pacific, and thence to Cathay.* There is no representation of the western sea, as shown on the Verrazano map, but on the contrary, the whole of the western coast of North America is shown conjecturally in a different form, by dotted lines. So far as this map affords any indication on the subject, it refers to the route of Cartier, and delineates the Atlantic coast according to the Spanish map of Ribero, that is, with a trending of the coast in a more northerly direction than the Verrazano map, and with the peculiar return of that coast westerly, in latitude 40° N., given on that map. The next chart (No. xv. *d*) from a map made by Diego Homem in 1540, shows the western sea nearly the same as on the map of Agnese, but conjecturally only; while the representation of the Atlantic coast has the same characteristics as the Bodleian and Agnese maps, showing its derivation from Ribero and not the Verrazano map. The remaining sketch given by Mr. Kohl (No. xv. *b*) from a map made by G. Ruscelli in 1544, presenting the same features, as do the two others, in regard to the Atlantic coast, puts beyond all question that the map of Ribero is its authority, by adopting from it the name of *Montagne Verde* which is applied by Ribero to the hills at the mouth of the river San Antonio, in latitude 41° N., thereby certainly excluding any recognition of the Verrazzano discovery or the Verrazano map.

The first published map which refers to the Verrazzano discoveries, that of Mercator in 1569, makes no reference to the Verrazano map, and does not recognize it in any manner. Mercator was the first to give the name of Claudia to the island of Louise, evidently mistaking the name of the wife of Francis for that of his mother, after whom the island was called, according to the letter, without stating her name. Mercator gives a legend in which he mentions that Verrazzano arrived on the coast on the 17th of March 1524, which is the day according to the version of Ramusio, following our mode of computation, as before explained. It is evident, therefore, that Mercator had the Ramusio version before him, and not the Verrazano map, as his authority on the subject. His delineation of the Atlantic coast, moreover, is according to the plan of Ribero, and he gives no indication of the western sea of the Verrazano map, but mentions in a legend the fresh water inland sea spoken of by Cartier, of the extent of which the Indians were ignorant.

The existence of the Verrazano map, much less its date, is obviously not proven by any of the maps or charts to which reference has here been made, and which are supposed to reflect some of its features, or indicate the verity of the Verrazzano discovery. There is, however, some evidence of a positive character, both historical and cartographical, which points to the existence of this map in two different forms, one originally not representing the Verrazzano discovery, and the other subsequently, as now presented.

The existence of a Verrazano map in some form or other, as early as 1537, seems to be established by a letter of the commendatory, Annibal Caro, written in that year. Caro, who became distinguished among his countrymen for his polite learning, was, in early life, secretary to the cardinal, M. de Gaddi, a Florentine, residing in Rome. While thus engaged, he accompanied his patron on a journey to the mines of Sicily, and there, from Castro, addressed a playful letter to the members generally of the cardinal's household, remaining at Rome. In this letter, which is dated the 13th of October in that year, he writes to them: " I will address sometimes one and sometimes another of you, as matters come into my mind. To you, Verrazzano, a seeker of *new worlds* and their marvels, I cannot yet say anything worthy of *your map*, because we have not passed through any country which has not been discovered by you or your brother."[1] This passage was supposed by Tiraboschi to have been addressed to the navigator, and as proving that he was alive at the time the letter was written. But we now know that Verrazzano had then been dead ten years; besides, it is not probable, inasmuch as the person addressed was one of the servants of the prelate, that the navigator would have occupied that position. M. Arcangeli suggests that the name is used by Caro merely as a *nom de guerre;*[2] but in either case, whether borrowed or not, the remark plainly enough refers to a Verrazzano map, which may *possibly* have been the map of Hieronimo.

---

[1] *De le lettre familiari del commendatore Annibal Caro*, vol. I. p. 6–7. Venetia 1581.

[2] *Discorso Sopra Giovanni da Verrazzano*, p. 27, in *Archivio Storico Italiano*, Appendice vol. IX.

Hakluyt furnishes testimony which, if correct, shows the probable existence of this map before 1529, *but not in its present form*. In the dedication to Phillip Sydney of his "Divers voyages touching the discoveries of America, &c.," printed in 1582, he refers to the probabilities of the existence of a northwest passage, and remarks that, "Master John Verarzanus which had been *thrise on that coast* in an olde excellent mappe, which *he gave* to King Henry the eight, and is yet in custodie of Master Locke, doth so lay it out as is to bee seene in the mappe annexed to the end of this boke, being made according to Verarzanus plat." Hakluyt thus positively affirms that the old map to which he refers was given by Verrazzano himself to the king. What evidence he had of that fact he does not mention, but he speaks of the map as if it had been seen by him, and probably that was his authority. The map he declares of his own knowledge was transferred, so far as regards the western strait, to the map of Lok, which he himself publishes. Lok's map represents the northwest passage as attempted by Frobisher in his several voyages, and as continued from the termination of the English exploration, to a western sea, a portion of which lying between the parallels of 40° N. and 50° N. latitude is laid down the same as it appears on the Verrazano map, and bears the inscription of *Mare de Verrazana* 1524. The map of Lok is the first one upon which the western sea is so called. The designation was undoubtedly the work of Lok himself, as it is in conformity with his practice in other parts of the map, where he denotes the discoveries of others in the same way, that is, by their names with the dates of their voyages annexed. He no doubt applied the name of Verrazzano to this ocean from finding it represented on the old map given by Verrazzano to the king, and obtained the date from the letter, of which Hakluyt printed in the same volume a translation from the version in Ramusio. It is certain that Verrazzano could not have been accessory to declaring it a *discovery* by himself for the reason already mentioned that no such sea, as there laid down, existed to have been discovered.

Lok's map represents on the Atlantic coast, in latitude 41° N., the island alleged in the Verrazzano letter to have been named after the king's mother, and gives it the name of Claudia. That it is the same island is proven by note to the translation of the letter given in the volume in which this map is found. Hakluyt puts in the margin, opposite the passage where mention of the island occurs in the letter, the words "Claudia Ilande." From whatever source this name was derived by them, whether from Mercator or by their own mistake, both Lok and Hakluyt here indirectly bear their testimony to the fact, that the name of Luisia was not upon the old map given to Henry VIII, which Lok consulted, and Hakluyt described. It is thus to be concluded that the map delivered to the king showed the western sea, but not any discoveries of Verrazzano on the Atlantic coast.

In another work, as yet unpublished, Hakluyt affords some additional information in regard to the old map, which though brief, is quite significant. He remarks that it is "a mightie large olde mappe in parchment, made *as it should seem* by Verrazanus, now in the custodie of Mr. Michael Locke;" and he speaks also of an "olde excellent *globe* in the Queen's privie gallery, at Westm'r, w'h *also seemeth* to be of Verrazanus making."[1] Both the map and the globe are thus mentioned as the *probable* workmanship of Verrazzano, from which it is probable that there was no name upon them to determine that question positively. The great size of the chart, the material upon which it was made, and the authorship of the map and globe by the same person, are circumstances which go to prove that they were both the work of a professed cosmographer, and embraced the whole world; and consequently that the map was not a chart made by the navigator, showing his discoveries, but possibly the map of Hieronimo in its original form. The construction of this old map, whoever was the author, is fixed certainly *before* 1529, by the statement of Hakluyt, that it was presented to Henry VIII by Verrazzano, the navigator, inasmuch as Verrazzano came to his death in 1527. The Verrazano map, in its present phase, not claiming to have been made before the year 1529, could not, therefore, have furnished the original representation of the western sea, or have been the one used by Lok.

Hakluyt adds to his statement that Verrazzano had been three times on the coast of America, which, if true, would disprove the discovery set up in the letter. That document alleges that the coast explored by him was entirely unknown and *had never before been seen by any one* before that voyage, and consequently not by him; and that, as regards the residue of the coast north

---

[1] MS. in possession of the Maine Historical Society, cited in Mr. Kohl's *Discovery of Maine*, p. 291, *note*.

of 50° N., the Portuguese had sailed along it as far as the Arctic circle, without finding any termination to the land, thus giving the Portuguese as his authority for the continuity of the northern part of the coast, and excluding himself from it. It is thus clearly stated in the letter, that he had not been there before. It was impossible that he could have consummated two voyages to America, and another to England, and made his court to the king, *after* 1524, and before his last and fatal cruize along the coast of Spain, as would have been necessary to have been done. In asserting that Verrazzano made other voyages to America, Hakluyt is corroborated by the ancient manuscripts, to which the author of the memoirs of Dieppe refers, as mentioning that one Jean Vérassen commanded a ship which accompanied that of Aubert to Newfoundland in 1508.[1] It is possible, therefore, that Verrazzano made three voyages to Newfoundland, and was well acquainted with that portion of the coast, before hostilities broke out between Francis I. and the emperor, in 1522; at which time, as will be seen, he entered upon his course of privateering; and that during the time Francis was a prisoner at Madrid, in 1525-6, and the state of war accordingly suspended, and Verrazzano thrown out of employment, he visited England, and laid before the king a scheme of searching for the northwest passage; a project which Henry had been long meditating, as may be gathered from

---

[1] Desmarquets. *Mémoires Chronologiques pour servir a l' histoire de Dieppe*, I. 100. (2 Vols. Paris, 1785.) It is worthy of remark that this annalist seems to regard Vérassen and Verrazzano as different persons, which proves, at least, that his authority was independent of any matter connected with the Verrazzano claim. That these names really relate, however, to the same individual, appears from the agreement with Chabot

the proposition of Wolsey to Sebastian Cabot in 1519, and the expedition actually sent out for that purpose by that monarch under John Rut, in 1527.[1] It is evident that the representation of the western sea, upon the map given to the king, was merely conjectural of its existence in connection with the supposed strait, laid down upon the map, according to Hakluyt. This explanation will serve also to account most readily for the partial knowledge which the letter exhibits, in regard to the customs and characteristics of the Indians of Cape Breton, which might have been collected by the writer, from the journals of those early voyages or other notes of Verrazzano in relation to them; although the same information was obtainable from others who had made similar voyages to that region, from Normandy and Brittany.

It is thus established by the same testimony which furnishes the map of Lok, taken in conjunction with its own teachings, that it was not derived from the Verrazano map in its present shape, and does not represent the Verrazzano discovery.

The only evidence of the existence of the Verrazano map in any cosmographical production whatever, book, chart or globe, so far as known, independently of its history in the Borgian collection, is a copper globe found by the late Buckingham Smith in Spain, a few years ago, and now in the possession of the New York Historical Society. This globe purports to have been constructed by Euphrosynus Ulpius in 1542.

---

[1] Letter of Contarini, the Venetian ambassador in Spain, to the Council of Ten. See *Calendar of State Papers &c. in Venice*, 1520-6. Edited by Rawdon Brown. No. 607. London, 1869. Purchas, III. p. 809.

Inscribed upon it, in a separate scroll, is a dedication, in these words: " Marcello Cervino S. R. E. Presbitero Cardinali D.D. Rome." Cervinus had been archbishop of Florence and was afterwards raised from the cardinalate to the pontificate under the title of Marcellus II. This globe represents the western sea in the same form as it is on the Verrazano map, and contains a legend on the country lying between the isthmus and Cape Breton, in these words: *Verrazana sive Nova Gallia a Verrazano Florentino Comperta anno sal. M.D.* In all other respects it differs essentially from the map in its description of the coast. Florida and Cape Breton are laid down in their true positions, and the isthmus occurs at the parallel of 33° N. latitude, instead of 41°. The direction of the coast, between the two points just mentioned, is more northerly, and the length of it consequently much reduced. The names along the coast, so far as the photograph of the map furnishes the means of comparison, are entirely different, except that Piaggia de Calami appears north of the isthmus. Dieppa and Livorno are not found upon it. But the legend affords indubitable evidence that the maker had consulted the map. The name of Verrazana applied to the land is found no where else so applied, except on the map. But the incompleteness in which the date of the discovery is left, as if written 15—, proves that the maker was unable to ascertain it fully from his authority; the map, therefore, must have been his sole authority.

As to the authenticity of this globe there is no other evidence than that it has the appearance of an old instrument, and its representations generally corre-

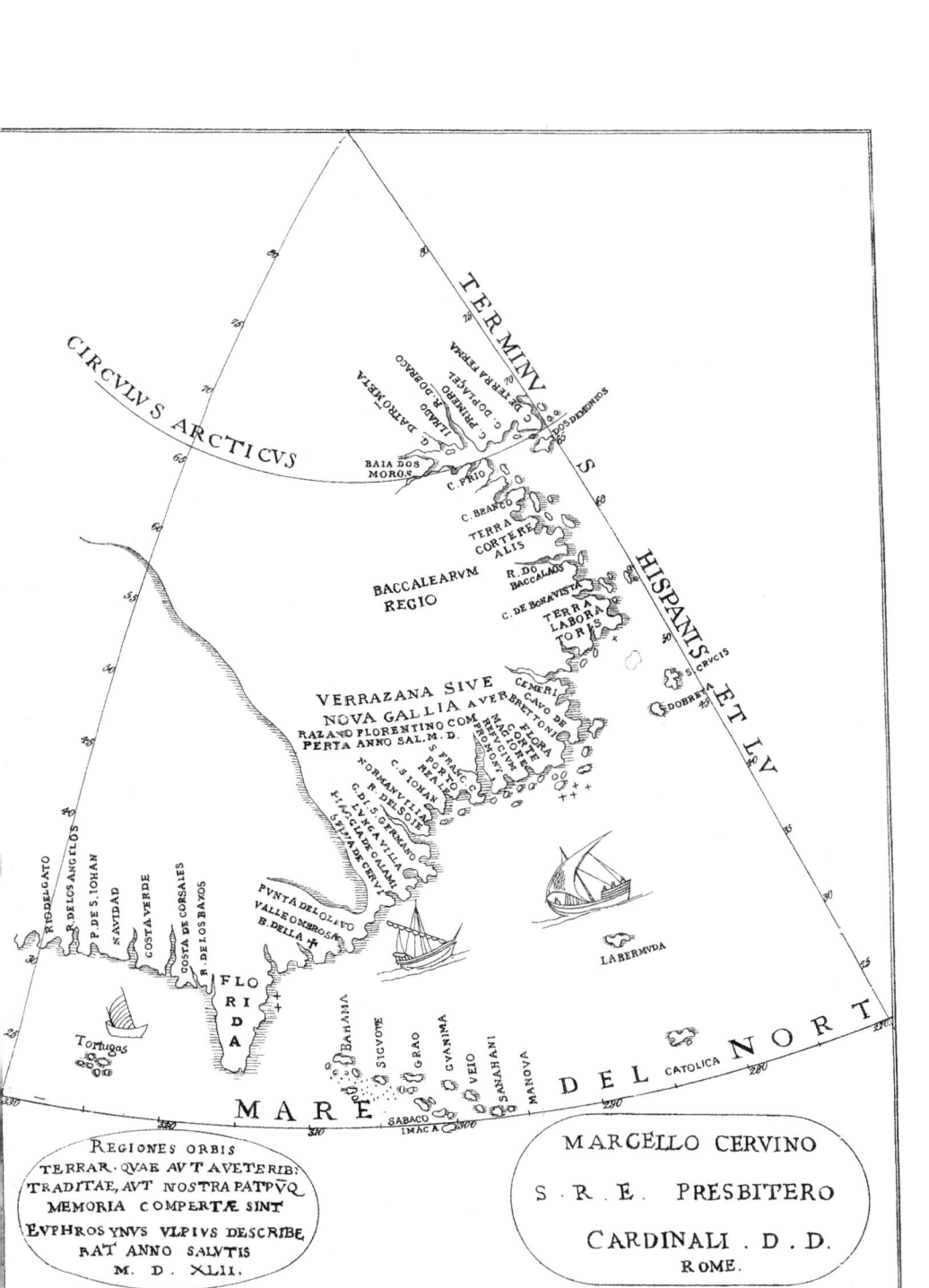

spond with the state of geographical knowledge of the period of its date.¹ Adopting its own story of its construction, it proves the existence of the Verrazano map, with the Verrazzano discoveries upon it, and consequently the existence of the claim as early as the year 1542.

The other references to a Verrazzano map, prove nothing on the subject of the discoveries, unless the letter of Annibal Caro, which alludes to discoveries by the brothers Verrazzani, in connection with a map, be deemed as referring to them. In that case, 1537 would be the earliest mention of them in any known publication. Lok and Hakluyt, as has been already seen, clearly do not refer to any map showing the Verrazzano discoveries. The period of the fabrication of the letter may therefore, possibly, be fixed between 1536 and 1542. But whether this period be properly deduced or not, is immaterial; since in no event can an earlier date than 1529 be assigned by any evidence outside of the letter, for the existence of the Verrazzano claim; which year, as is now to be shown, was long after the coast had been discovered and made known to the world by another.

---

¹ It measures forty-two inches in circumference. *Hist. Mag.* (New York) 1862, p. 202. A map showing so much of it as relates to North America, was lithographed for the dissertation of Mr. Smith, and is here reproduced.

IX.

THE LETTER TO THE KING FOUNDED ON THE DISCOVERIES OF ESTÉVAN GOMEZ. THE HISTORY OF GOMEZ AND HIS VOYAGE. THE PUBLICATION OF HIS DISCOVERIES IN SPAIN AND ITALY BEFORE THE VERRAZZANO CLAIM. THE VOYAGE DESCRIBED IN THE LETTER TRACED TO RIBERO'S MAP OF THE DISCOVERIES OF GOMEZ.

In the proofs adduced, outside of the letter addressed to the king, no direct evidence appears in regard to the discovery. There is no testimony to be found of any one who took part in the setting forth or equipment of the expedition, or in the prosecution of the voyage, or who was personally cognizant of the return of the Dauphiny. No chart or private letter, no declaration or statement of the navigator, in regard to the extraordinary discovery achieved by him, is produced or mentioned, although he belonged to a family of some note in Tuscany, which still existed in the present century. In this respect, Italy, the birth place and home of Verrazzano, is as blank and barren as France. All that is really shown of any pertinency is the single circumstance, that possibly the claim to the discovery was advanced in Italy, and in that country alone, at the time of the construction of the globe of Ulpius in 1542, but not anterior to the year 1529, or until five years after the event, when, according to the Verrazano map, if that be accepted as genuine in its present form, and the most favorable construction be upon its ambiguous legend, of which that inscription is capable, the claim was for the first time announced. And thus there is nothing showing that the letter or its pretensions were known before the last named year. In view of this important fact, and the absence of any evidence whatsoever corroborative of the letter or its contents, it is not unreasonable to believe that the letter was an attempt to appropriate to the Florentine the glory which belonged to Estévan Gomez, a Portuguese pilot, who actually discovered and explored this coast, in 1525, in the service of the emperor, Charles V, and whose voyage and exploration were immediately thereupon made known, both in Spain and Italy. That such, indeed, was the source from which the Verrazzano letter was derived is susceptible of demonstration; and for that purpose some account of the voyage and discoveries of Gomez and their publication becomes necessary.

Gomez, who was born in Oporto and reared there to a sea-faring life, for some reason, unexplained, left Portugal and entered into the Spanish service, in which he was appointed pilot in 1518, at the same time that Sebastian Cabot was created pilot major in the same service. He proposed immediately to the king, to go in search of a new route to the Moluccas or Spice islands recently discovered by the Portuguese, and which, he affirmed, were within the limits assigned to Spain by the line of demarkation. He exhibited a chart constructed by him showing this fact,[1] from which it may be inferred that he had already made a voyage to

---
[1] Cespedes, *Regimiento de Navigacion*, 148.

those islands. The way which he proposed then to take is not mentioned. At the same juncture Magellan also arrived in Spain and tendered his services to find a new route to the Moluccas, specifically by the west, as delineated on a globe which he produced. Magellan prevailed in his suit, which was the reason, according to Pigafetta, the historian of the expedition, that the emperor did not give Gomez any caravels to discover new lands.[1] It is to be inferred, therefore, that the first route proposed by Gomez was not by the west. The fleet of Magellan set sail on his expedition in September 1519, with Gomez as chief pilot, an arrangement intended to conciliate and combine both interests; but it was not a happy one. Actuated, it is charged, by a spirit of jealousy and a desire to embarrass Magellan and render his voyage abortive, Gomez at the very moment that success was assured, and the fleet was entering the strait which led into the Pacific, abandoned his commander; and profiting by the opportunity which was offered him in being detached by Magellan with the San Antonio, one of the ships, to make a reconnoissance in another direction, joined with certain mutineers, seized the captain of that vessel, and returned with her to Spain, arriving there in March 1521. The reasons assigned by him for this desertion of the expedition, were the severity of the treatment of the crew by Magellan, a want of provisions and the unseaworthiness of the San Antonio. He was, however, held by the council of the Indies to answer to any charges which might be preferred against him by Magellan on his return, and in the meantime his pay

---

[1] *Primo Viaggio*, 38.

was sequestered and his property on board the ship attached. In September 1522, the Victoria, the only ship of Magellan's squadron which succeeded in returning to Spain, arrived with the news of Magellan's discovery, and also of his death in a conflict with the natives of the island of Tidore. Upon this information proceedings against Gomez were discontinued and his property released.

The success of Magellan served the more to stimulate the purpose of Gomez to undertake a search for the same object. It was supposed at that time, by Sebastian Cabot and others, that the northern parts of America were broken up into islands, but nothing positively was known in relation to them, except in the region of Newfoundland. Between that country and South Carolina, then recently discovered by the joint expedition of the licentiates, all was unknown; and it was considered not improbable that a passage might be found between those points, through to Cathay and the Moluccas, the same as had been discovered in the south, by Magellan. Gomez, released from his disabilities, renewed his application to the emperor for permission to prosecute his search, proposing now to make it through the northern seas; and on the 27th of August 1523 a cedule was made to that effect authorizing him to go with a caravel of fifty toneles burden " on the discovery of eastern Cathay.[1] In consequence, however, of the remonstrance of the king of Portugal against any interference with his rights to the Moluccas, Charles suspended the prosecution of further voyages in that quarter until the question

---

[1] Herrera, III. IV. 20. The cedule is still extant in the archives at Seville.

should be determined to which of the two crowns those islands belonged by virtue of the pope's demarcation. The voyage of Gomez, and also that of Cabot to the La Plata, were delayed until the decision of the junta convened at Badajos by the two monarchs for the purpose of making this determination. To this body Gomez, in conjunction with Sebastian Cabot and Juan Vespucci as pilots, and Diego Ribero as cartographer, was attached,— a circumstance which shows the high estimation in which his nautical knowledge was held. Its proceedings closed in May 1524, too late for Gomez to make his arrangements to leave in that year. These were completed, however, in February 1525, in which month he set sail from Coruña, in the north of Spain, in a single caravel, on his voyage of discovery.[1] Peter Martyr, after mentioning the proposed expedition of Sebastian Cabot to the south, thus refers in July 1524, to that of Gomez and its destination. " It is also decreed that one Stephanus Gomez, who also himselfe is a skillful navigator, shal goe another way, whereby, betweene the Baccalaos and Florida, long since our countries, he saith he will finde out a waye to Cataia: one onely shippe, called a Carvell, is furnished for him, and he shall have no other thing in charge then to search out whether any passage to the great Chan, from out the diuers windings and vast compassings of this our *Ocean*, were to be founde." [2]

Gomez commenced his exploration on the coast of South Carolina, and proceeding thence northwardly, reached the *Rio de la buelta*, where, as that name de-

---

[1] Navarrete III. 179. Peter Martyr, Dec. VIII. 8.
[2] Peter Martyr, *Dec.* VI. 10. *Eden's trans.*

notes, he commenced his return, on the island of Cape Breton. He carefully observed the rivers, capes and bays, which occur within those limits, entering the Chesapeake, Delaware, Hudson and Penobscot, to which he gave appropriate names, derived from the church calendar, or from some characteristic of the locality. He was for a while encouraged to believe, in consequence of the great flood of water which he found issuing from the Penobscot, or *Rio de Gamos*, (Stag river), that he had there fallen upon the desired strait. Though unsuccessful in the object of his search, he nevertheless accomplished an important service for geographical science, in determining that no such passage existed within the region he had sailed. Taking in a cargo of Indians from the islands of the great bay, he continued his course to the south, and running along the coast of Florida, returned to Spain by way of Cuba.[1]

The authenticity of this voyage is established by Oviedo and Peter Martyr both of whom were eyewitnesses of the Indians which Gomez brought home and exhibited at Toledo. Both of these writers have given short accounts of the voyage, which, as it was not successful in the purpose for which it was undertaken and promised no returns of gold, excited no public attention. The results were, however, interesting to the hydrographers of Spain, who soon prepared charts of the coast, according to his exploration, among which

---

[1] Peter Martyr, *Dec.* VI. c. 10. Herrera, III. VIII. 8. Cespedes, *Yslario General*, in MS. Cespedes was cosmographer major of the Indies in Seville and wrote many geographical works early in the seventeenth century. His *Yslario General*, embracing a history of the islands of the world, exists in the Biblioteca Nacional in Madrid.

that made by Diego Ribero, associate of Gomez at the junta of Badajos, and royal cosmographer, will demand especial attention.

The voyage of Gomez and what he had accomplished became immediately known to the world at large by printed publications. He arrived home on his return in November 1525; and three months afterwards Oviedo published his first work, addressed to the emperor, in which he makes the following brief mention of the expedition.

"Shortly after that yowr Maiestie came to the citie of Toledo, there arryved in the moneth of November, Stephen Gomes the pylot who the yeare before of 1524 by the commandement of yowre maiestie sayled to the Northe partes and founde a greate parte of lande continuate from that which is cauled Baccaleos discoursynge towarde the West to the XL, and XLI degree, frō whense he brought certeyne Indians, of the whiche he brought sum with hym from thense who are yet in Toledo at this present, and of greater stature than other of the firme land as they are commonlye. Theyr coloure is much like the other of the firme lande. They are great archers, and go couered with the skinnes of dyuers beastes both wylde and tame. In this lande are many excellent furres, as marterns, sables and such other rych furres, of the which the sayde pilot brought summe with hym into Spayne. They have sylver and copper and certeyne other metalles. They are Idolaters and honoure the soonne and moone, and are seduced with suche superstitions and errours as are they of the firme." [1]

The details of the exploration appear more distinctly upon the charts which the royal cosmographers at Seville prepared, with the names given to the prominent points of the coast. Two of these maps are still extant, bearing the respective dates of 1527

---

[1] *Oviedo de la natural hystoria de las Indias.* (Toledo, 15 Feby. 1526), fol. 14; and under the title of *Relacion Sumaria*, p. 16, in Barcia's *Historiadores primitivos*, tome I. Translated in Eden's *Decades of the newe worlde*, fol. 213-14.

THE LETTER FOUNDED ON THE VOYAGE OF GOMEZ. 123

and 1529, the first by an anonymous cartographer, and the last by Ribero.[1] The whole line of coast from the river Jordan, in latitude 33° 10', visited by both the expeditions of Ayllon, to Cape Breton, is laid down upon them with sufficient exactitude. The names indicate the exploration to have been made by Gomez the whole distance between those points; for no other navigator of Spain, in the language of which they are given, had sailed within those limits up to the time these maps bear date. The only question which has been raised in this regard relates to the expeditions of Ayllon; but the first of these, a joint descent upon the coast to carry off Indians in 1520 by two vessels belonging to the licentiates Ayllon and Matienzo of St. Domingo, proceeded no further than the Jordan, as we learn from the testimony of Pedro de Quejo, the pilot of Matienzo.[2] The expedition which Ayllon made afterwards in 1526, in person, to the same coast, proceeded directly to the river Jordan, and after remaining there a few days, ran southwesterly along the coast to Gualdape or St Helena, where Ayllon died, and from whence it thereupon immediately returned home to St Domingo, without any further attempt at exploration.[3]

---

[1] Both these maps, so far as they relate to America, have been reproduced, with very valuable notes and illustrations, by Mr. Kohl in *Die beiden altesten general karten von America*. Weimar, 1860.

[2] Proceedings before the Auditors at St Domingo, by virtue of a royal decree, of Nov. 1525, in relation to the dispute between Ayllon and Matienzo concerning their discovery, preserved in MS. at Seville.

[3] Oviedo, tom. III. p. 624. (Madrid, 1853,) Mr. Kohl states (*Discovery of Maine*, 397) that the ships of Ayllon made an extensive survey of the coast, *north* of the Jordan, soon after their arrival in the country. In this he is in error; into which he appears to have been misled by Navarrete, a part of whose language he quotes in a note, as that of Oviedo. Navarrete,

This disastrous expedition, therefore, went no further north than the Jordan or Santee. It demonstrated the falsity of the stories told to Peter Martyr by Francis, the Chicorane, as he was called, one of the Indians seized in the first expedition and taken by Ayllon to Spain, of the vast provinces with uncouth names which were upon his authority transferred to the royal cedule granted to Ayllon on the 12th June, 1523.[1] That region remained unknown, therefore, until the voyage of Gomez, and to it and it alone can the names on these maps, within the limits before designated, be attributed.

These maps passed at once into Italy; and that of Ribero, bearing the date of 1529 and the arms of the then reigning pontiff, Clement VII, and his successors, the most finished of the three copies known to exist, is still to be found at Rome, and is reasonably supposed to have been the original; and like

referring to the portion of Oviedo's history, not then (1829) published, as his authority, says on this point that after leaving the river Jordan the ships of Ayllon proceeded to Gualdape, "distante cuarenta ó cincuenta leguas mas *al norte*" *distant forty or fifty leagues more to the north;* whereas the language of Oviedo, as contained in the recently published edition of his work, is, "acordaron de yrse á poblar la costa delante háçia la costa *occidental*, é fueron a un grand rio (quarenta ó quarenta é çinco leguas de alli, pocas más ó menos) que se diçe Gualdape," (ut supra, p. 628) *they agreed to go and settle the coast further on towards the west coast, and went to a large river, (forty or forty-five leagues from that place, a little more or less) which is called Gualdape.* The course of the coast at these points is northeast and southwest. A westerly course was therefore to the *south* and not to the north. Besides, Oviedo states that the Jordan was in latitude 33° 40′ and that Gualdape was the country through which the river St. Helena ran, which he also calls the river of Gualdape, and which in another part of his history he places in latitude 33° N., and expressly stating that the Jordan was north of the St. Helena, towards Cape Trafalgar, or Cape Fear (tom. II. p. 144.) Ayllon, therefore, did not sail north of the Jordan, and the names on the Ribero map, north of that river, are not attributable to his expedition.

[1] P. Martyr, Dec. VII. c. 2; Navarrete, III. 153.

the last decade of Peter Martyr in 1526, which mentions the discoveries of Gomez, to have been sent to the Holy Father at his desire, in order to keep him informed of the latest discoveries.[1] Other copies of the Spanish charts showing the exploration of Gomez, found their way into Italy about the same time, proving that there was then no interdict against their exportation from Spain to that country, at least.[2] This appears by a volume which was published in Venice in 1534 under the auspices of Ramusio,[3] embracing a summary of the general history of the West Indies by Peter Martyr and a translation of Oviedo's natural history of the Indies of 1526, containing the account of Gomez' voyage, with a map of America upon which the discoveries of Gomez are laid down the same as upon the Spanish maps of 1527 and 1529, before mentioned. The following colophon, giving the origin of this map, is to be found at the end of the translation of Oviedo: "Printed at Venice, in the month of December 1534. For the explanation of these books there has been made an universal map of the countries of all the West Indies, together with a special map, taken from two marine charts of the Spaniards, one of which belonged to Don Pietro Martire, Councillor of the Royal Council

---

[1] *Nouvelles Annales des Voyages.* Nouvelle series, tome xxxv. Année 1853. Tome troisieme. Paris. *Les Papes géographes et la cartographie du Vatican.* Par R. M. Thomassey. Appendix, p. 275.

[2] In regard to the freedom which the charts of the Spanish navigators so enjoyed there is confirmatory proof in Ramusio. In the preface to his third volume, dedicated to his friend Fracastor of Florence, he writes: "All the literary men daily inform you of any discovery made known to them by captain or pilot coming from those parts, and among others the aforesaid Sig. Gonzalo (Oviedo) from the island of Hispaniola, who every year visits you once or twice with some new made chart."

[3] M. d'Avezac in *Bulletin de la Societé de Géographie* for July and August 1872.

of the said Indies, and was made by the pilot and master of marine charts, Niño Garzia de Loreno, in Seville. The other was made also by a pilot of the majesty, the emperor, in Seville. With which maps the reader can inform himself of the whole of this new world, place by place, the same as if he had been there himself."[1] The special map here referred to is one of Hispaniola, in the same volume, and was undoubtedly taken from that of Nuño Garcia, in the possession of Peter Martyr. It was therefore made in or before the year 1526, since Martyr died in that year. The map of America, by the pilot of the emperor at Seville, was probably the anonymous map of 1527 before mentioned, as it appears not to have had the name of the author upon it. These facts prove at least that the map of Ribero was in Italy in the year 1529, and that the map of 1527 may have been there before that year.

It was from the delineation of the coast on one or other of these two maps, which are in that respect almost identically the same, that the description of it in the Verrazzano letter was derived. This will now be made manifest by the application of that description to the map of Ribero, so much of which as is necessary, is here reproduced for that purpose.

In making the proof thus proposed, it is to be borne in mind that the letter is positive and explicit as to the extent and limits of the discovery or exploration which it describes. It fixes them by three different modes which prove each other: 1. By giving the latitude

---

[1] This volume has no general title, but contains three books, *primo, secondo & ultimo della historia de l' Indie Occidentali.* It is very rarely found with the large map of America. We are indebted to the kindness of James Lenox, Esq., of New York, for the use of a perfect copy in this respect.

THE LETTER FOUNDED ON THE VOYAGE OF GOMEZ. 127

of the commencement and termination of the voyage along the coast; 2. By a declaration in two different forms of the entire distance run, and 3. By a statement of intermediate courses and distances, from point to point, between the landfall and the place of leaving the coast, separately, making in the aggregate the whole distance named. There can be therefore no mistake as to the meaning of the writer in respect of the extent of the exploration.

As to its limits and extent, we have already had occasion to quote his language in impressing upon Francis the great length of the voyage; giving both at the same time: "In the voyage," he says, "which we made by order of your majesty, in addition to the 92 degrees which we ran towards the west from our point of departure, before we reached land *in latitude 34, we have to count 300 leagues which we ran northeastwardly and 400 nearly east, along the coast, before we reached the 50th parallel of north latitude,* the point where we turned our course from the shore towards home." This distance is also mentioned in the total at the end of the voyage, where he says: "finding our provisions and naval stores nearly exhausted, we took in wood and water, and determined to return to France, having discovered 700 leagues of unknown lands."

The several courses and distances run are described in the letter, from point to point, as follows:[1]

First. "We perceived that it (the land) stretched to the *south* and coasted along in that direction in search of

---

[1] The translation of Dr. Cogswell, in *N. Y. Hist. Collections*, is here used, somewhat condensed.

some port in which we might come to anchor, and examine into the nature of the country, but for *fifty leagues* we could find none in which we could lie securely."

L. 50

Second. "Seeing the coast still stretched to the south we resolved to change our course and stand to the northward, and as we still had the same difficulty, we drew in with the land, and sent a boat ashore. Many people, who were seen coming to the sea-side, fled at our approach. We found not far from this people another. This country is plentifully supplied with lakes and ponds of running water, and being in the latitude of 34, the air is salubrious, pure and temperate, and free from the extremes both of heat and cold. We set sail from this place continuing to coast along the shore, which we found stretching out to the west (east?). While at anchor on this coast, there being no harbor to enter, we sent the boat on shore with twenty-five men to obtain water. Departing hence, and always following the shore, which stretched to the *north*, we came in the space of *fifty leagues*, to another land which appeared beautiful and full of the largest forests."

50

Third. "After having remained here three days riding at anchor on the coast, as we could find no harbor we determined to depart, and coast along the shore to the *northeast*. After proceeding *one hundred leagues*, we found a very pleasant situation among *some steep hills through which a very large river*, deep at its mouth forced its way to the sea."

100

Fourth. "We took the boat and entering the river we found the country on its banks well peopled. All of a sudden a violent contrary wind blew in from the sea, and forced us to return to our ship. Weighing anchor, we sailed *eighty leagues towards the east*, as the coast stretched in that direction, and always in sight of it. At length we discovered an island, triangular in form, about ten leagues from the mainland. We gave it the name of your majesty's illustrious mother."

80

Fifth. "We did not land there, as the weather was unfavorable, but proceeded to another place, *fifteen leagues* distant from the island, where we found a very excellent harbor. It looks towards the south, on which side the harbor is half a league broad. Afterwards, upon entering it, the extent between the east and the north is twelve leagues, and

THE LETTER FOUNDED ON THE VOYAGE OF GOMEZ. 129

then enlarging itself, forms a *very large bay*, twenty leagues in circumference."   15

Sixth. "Having supplied ourselves with every thing necessary, on the sixth of May we departed from the port and sailed one hundred and fifty leagues, keeping so close to the coast as never to lose it from our sight. *We did not stop to land*, as the weather was very favorable for pursuing our voyage, and the country presented no variety. The shore stretched to the *east*"   150

Seventh. "And *fifty leagues* beyond, *more to* the *north*, where we found a *more elevated country*. The people were entirely different from the others we had seen, so rude and barbarous that we were unable by any signs we could make, to hold communication with them. Against their will *we penetrated two or three leagues into the interior* with twenty-five men."   50

Eighth. "Departing from thence we kept along the coast, steering *between east and north*, and found the country more pleasant and open. Within *fifty leagues* we discovered thirty two islands, all near the mainland."   50

Ninth. "We had no intercourse with the people. After sailing between east and north *one hundred and fifty leagues more* we determined to return to France, having discovered 700 leagues of unknown lands."   150

Making a total of   695 L.

Now let the reader trace for himself, these courses and distances, as shown on the accompanying sketch of the map of Ribero, according to the following scale,

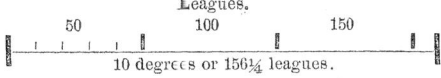

representing the measurements in the letter; which are calculated on the basis of 15.625 leagues to a degree, while those on the map are $17\frac{1}{2}$ leagues; and he will find, that not only is the whole littoral distance between the parallels of 34° and 50° on the map about seven hundred leagues, but that the several courses and distances, of which this entire distance is composed according to the letter, correspond with similar divisions on the map, proving to a certainty that this map was the source from which the line of coast described in the letter was derived, or the reverse.

It will be observed that the *first* course, beginning according to the letter at the landfall, in latitude 34 N., commences on the map a little north of *C. Traffalgar* as there laid down, now Cape Fear, and proceeds southerly fifty leagues to *C. de S. Roman*.

The first course being retraced, the *second*, also of fifty leagues, starting from the landfall near *C. Traffalgar*, extends to *C. de S. Juan* of the map, the well known point of Hatteras.

The *third*, runs from *C. de S. Juan*, one hundred leagues *northwardly*, to the *Montana verde*, the Navesinks at the mouth of the Hudson, "described as the pleasant situation among steep hills, through which a very large river forced its way into the sea." The perfect identification of this course and distance has already been observed.

The fourth extends *easterly* from the *Montana verde* eighty leagues and strikes the islands of the *C. de Muchas yllas*, or Cape Cod, where, among the Elizabeth islands, Martha's Vineyard and Nantucket, the island of Louise is intended by the letter to be placed. This course, easterly, fixes the position of that island at this point.

The *fifth* course and distance embrace fifteen leagues from the islands of *C. de Muchas yllas*, but the direction is not stated, and is left to be inferred from the fact which is stated that they proceeded on to another place where they entered a harbor, at the mouth of a large bay opening between *north* and east, of twelve leagues in width. This course must therefore have been *northerly* and proceeded along the easterly shore of *C. de Muchas yllas* or Cape Cod.

The sixth runs easterly from the harbor on the *C. de Muchas yllas*, or Cape Cod, one hundred and fifty leagues *easterly* which include the opening of the great bay of twelve leagues and proceeds along the *Arecifes* or C. Sable on the coast of Nova Scotia to the *Sarçales*, probably Cape Canso at Chedabucto bay, *where the coast trended more northerly.*

The *seventh*, from the *Sarçales*, fifty leagues *more to the north*, extends along the *tierra de los Bretones* or island of C. Breton to the cape of that name, passing the *R. de la buelta*, the easterly limit of the voyage of Gomez. From this river easterly the map is compiled, as the names indicate, from Portuguese charts.

The *eighth*, from C. Breton *fifty leagues* between north and east, runs along the easterly coast of the *tierra de los Bretones*, to the supposed northerly shore of the bay between that land and the *tierra de los Bacallaos* or Newfoundland, but in reality the southerly entrance into the gulf of St. Lawrence.

The *ninth*, from the termination of the last course, embraces one hundred and fifty leagues between north and east along the coast of the *Bacallaos* to *C. Rasso* or Cape Race and thence along the easterly coast of the Bacallaos to the Y. de Bacallaos in latitude 50° N., the point of departure from the coast, and making the complement of 695 leagues, in all.

Such exact and unexceptional concurrence in the

observation of distances for over two thousand miles, as this comparison exhibits, by two different navigators sailing at different times, under different circumstances of wind and weather, and under different plans of exploration, is impossible. So far as regards the distances running north and south, such an agreement might happen, because the truth in that direction was ascertainable by any one, by means of observations of the latitude; but not as regards those running east and west; for these, no means of determining them existed, as before explained: and accordingly on the Ribero map they are grossly incorrect. From the Montana verde to the C. de Muchas yllas, that is, from the Hudson to the west end of the peninsula of Cape Cod, the distance appears to be eighty leagues, or nearly double its true length; while the width of the great bay between the C. de Muchas yllas and the Arecifes, or from Cape Cod to Cape Sable is shown to be less than twenty leagues, whereas it is more than fifty. And so also from the Arecifes to the Sarçales, from Cape Sable to Cape Canso, it is one hundred and thirty-five leagues on the map, or twice the actual distance. These great errors show how impossible it was at that time to calculate longitudinal distances correctly. But two navigators, sailing independently as mentioned, could not have fallen into these errors exactly to the same extent, exaggerated in the two cases by the same excessive length, and in the other by the same extraordinary diminution. Yet in the particulars just described the map and the letter correspond precisely. Such a coincidence of mistakes, could not have been accidental.

One of these documents must, therefore, have been

the source of the other. In determining between them there can be no mistake in adopting as the original, that one which has a certain and indisputable authenticity, and rejecting that which is unsupported by any other testimony. The voyage of Gomez was long the subject of consideration and preparation, and was heralded to the world for months before it was undertaken. The order of the king of Spain under which it was made, still exists in the archives of that kingdom. The results of the expedition were announced by credible historians of the country, immediately after its return; and the nautical information which it brought back, and in regard to which alone it possessed any interest at the time, was transferred at once to the marine charts of the nation, imperfectly it is true, and spread before the world. These charts still remain in their original form, as they were then prepared. With these incontrovertible facts to sustain it, the discovery of Gomez must stand as established in history and, consequently, the claim of Verrazzano must fall.[1]

---

[1] The map of Ribero is not a faithful representation of the exploration of Gomez, in many respects. The *tierra de Ayllon* is made to embrace a large portion of the country the coast of which was discovered by Gomez. The bay of Santa Maria, or the Chesapeake, is placed two degrees further south than it should be, that is, in latitude 35°, instead of 37° N. The *R. de los Gamos*, or Penobscot, mentioned by Cespedes, is not named at all. The question, however, of its greater or less correctness is of no importance on the present occasion; it is sufficient that it was followed by the writer of the letter, erroneous as it was.

X.

THE CAREER OF VERRAZZANO. AN ADVENTUROUS LIFE AND AN IGNOMINIOUS DEATH. CONCLUSION.

The true history of Verrazzano, so far as known, is now to be given, in order to make a final disposition of this story. Nothing is preserved in relation to his early life. Even the year of his birth is matter of conjecture. He is called by Ramusio, Giovanni da Verrazzano, Florentine; and according to Pelli, was born about the year 1485. His father was Piero Andrea, son of Bernardo, the son of Bernardo of Verrazzano, a little town situated in the Val di Greve, near Florence,—the latter Bernardo having belonged to the magistracy of the priors in 1406. All that his eulogist was enabled to gather concerning him, beyond this brief genealogy, is taken from the Verrazzano letter and the discourse of Ramusio, relating how he was killed, roasted and devoured by the savages in a second voyage to America;[1] with the suggestion of

---

[1] The account which Ramusio gives of Verrazzano, and the manner of his death, occurs in his *Discourse on Labrador, the Baccalaos and New France* (vol. III. fol. 417), in which, after referring to the Cortereaes and Sebastian Cabot, he adds :

"There also sailed along the said land, in the year 1524, a great captain of the most Christian king in France, called Giovanni da Verrazzano, a Florentine ; and he ran along all the coast, as far as Florida, as will be particularly seen by a letter of his, written to the said king, which alone we have been able to have, because the others have got astray in the troubles of the unfortunate city of Florence. And in the last voyage which he made, having wished to descend on the land with some companions, they were all put to death by those people, and in the presence of those who remained on board of the ship, were roasted and devoured. Such a wretched

Coronelli, the Venetian geographer, that the place where he thus met his death was at the entrance of the gulf of St. Lawrence. The spurious letter of Carli adds that he had been in Egypt, Syria and most other parts of the world. The ancient manuscripts of Dieppe, as we have seen,[1] speak of one of his name who ac-

---

end had this valiant gentleman, who, had not this misfortune intervened, would, by the great knowledge and intelligence which he had of maritime affairs, and of navigation, accompanied and favoured by the immense liberality of King Francis, have discovered and made known to the world, all that part of the earth, up to the north pole, and would not have been contented with the coast merely, but would have sought to penetrate far inland, and as far as he could go; and many, who have known and conversed with him, have told me, that he declared it was his intention to seek to persuade the Most Christian King to send from these parts, a good number of people to settle in some places of said coast which are of temperate climate, and very fertile soil, with very beautiful rivers and harbors capable of holding any fleets. The settlers in these places would be the occasion of producing many good results, and among others of bringing those rude and ignorant tribes to divine worship, and to our most holy faith, and to show them how to cultivate the land, transporting some of the animals of our Europe to those vast plains; and finally, in time, having discovered the inland parts, and seen whether among the many islands existing there, any passage to the south sea exists, or whether the main land of Florida or the West Indies continues up to the pole. This and so much is what has been related of this so brave a gentleman, of whose toil and sweat, in order that his memory may not remain buried, and his name pass into oblivion, we have desired to give to the light the little that has come into our hands."

Ramusio here distinctly asserts that the only document in relation to the voyage of Verrazzano which he had been able to procure, was the letter which he published; but he informs his readers that he had been told by certain persons who had known and conversed with Verrazzano, that it was the intention of the navigator, as he himself declared, to seek permission from Francis I, his adopted sovereign, in whose service it is claimed he made the discovery, to make another voyage to the new found land for the purposes of colonization and further exploration; and he also states, upon the same or other authority, that Verrazzano on another voyage was killed and eaten, by the natives of the country. Consequently, Verrazzano must have made a second voyage to America and obtained such permission from the king. But there is not a particle of evidence in existence, apart from the declarations of these persons to Ramusio, that any such permission was ever given, or that a second voyage took place. It proves the credulity of Ramusio that he received these naked statements without any examination.

[1] *Ante*, p. 112, *note*.

companied Aubert, in his voyage to Newfoundland, in 1508; and the statement of Hakluyt before referred to, gives some ground to believe that he was employed in early voyages to that region, before he engaged in his operations against the commerce of Spain.

What is certainly known of him relates almost exclusively to his career as a French corsair, during the few years which intervened between the breaking out of hostilities between Francis I and Charles V, and his death, in 1527. His cruises, though directed principally against the Spaniards, were not tender of the interests of Portugal; and it is accordingly from Spanish and Portuguese writers and documents of the period, that the little information that exists in relation to him, is derived. He is called by the former, Juan Florin or Florentin, or simply, the Florentine,—the French corsair. He is designated on an occasion to be noted, as Juan Florin of *Dieppe*.[1] They appear to have known him by no other name. They never heard of him as a discoverer, real or pretended, of new countries, until long afterwards. The Verrazzano letter had not been published when Peter Martyr, Oviedo and Gomara wrote; and when Martyr and Gomara make mention of him, they do so only by the title by which he was designated by the Spanish sailors. There was, therefore, no opportunity for his identification by them in the double character of a great discoverer, and a corsair; and it was not until many years after the publication of the Verrazzano letter that this identification was first declared by Barcia.[2]

---

[1] On the capture of the treasure fleet. See *Appendix*, IV.

[2] *Ensayo Chronologico, sub anno,* 1524.

THE LIFE AND DEATH OF VERRAZZANO. 137

There is no room, however, to doubt its entire correctness. That the occupation of Verrazzano was that of a cruizer on the seas, is not only declared in the letter ascribed to him,[1] but is clearly established by the agreement made by him with Chabot. Besides, there is no other Giovanni, a Florentine, known in the history of the time, sailing in that capacity under the French flag and from the same port of Dieppe; and the references must have therefore been to him alone.

The appellation of corsair, does not necessarily imply a pirate. It was applicable to any one engaged in the capture of vessels on the high seas, whether authorized to do so or not. The state of hostilities between France and Spain, protected Verrazzano under the rules of war, as a subject of Francis, in capturing Spanish vessels, as long as it continued; and the an-

---

[1] Ramusio gives Verrazzano this character more distinctly than it appears in the original version. One of his first alterations of the text, is of the passage previously referred to, relating to the cruise of the Normandy and Dauphiny, after their repairs in Brittany. The Carli version reads, in connection with the two ships on that occasion: *dove restaurati ara V. S. M. inteso il discorso facemo con quelle armate in guerra per li liti di Spagna,* that is, "where being repaired, your serene majesty will have understood we made *the* cruize with *this fleet of war* along the coasts of Spain," from which it is to be implied only, that the cruize was for the purpose of depredating on Spanish commerce. But Ramusio, as became his practice, with this document at least, altered this clause into, *dove poi che furono secondo il bisogno raccōciate & ben armeggiate, per i liti di Spagna ce n'andammo in corso, il che V. M. haverà inteso per il profitto che ne facemmo;* which Hakluyt fairly renders: "where, after we had repaired them in all points as was needfull, and armed them very well, we took our course along by the coast of Spain, which your Majesty shall understand, *by the profit we received thereby.*" As this cruize according to the date of the letter must have taken place in 1523, this language, which is Ramusio's own, as to the profit, would seem to refer almost to the capture by Verrazzano of the treasure sent by Cortes, to the emperor which occurred in the summer of that year, as hereafter related; but Verrazzano's fleet consisted of six instead of two ships on that occasion. The words of Ramusio, show, however, that he knew Verrazzano was a rover, in search of booty on the seas, or at least, that he so regarded him.

omalous condition of affairs existing at that time, according to the Portuguese historian, Andrade, of private war between the subjects of the kings of France and Portugal, without any public war between the sovereigns, would seem to have justified him in similar acts in regard to the commerce of the Portuguese, as long as the practice was not forbidden by the kings of the two countries.

The first adventure of the kind, in which we hear of Verrazzano, was in 1521. At this time a valuable commerce had grown up between Spain and her conquests in the West Indies, and large amounts in gold, pearls, sugar, hides and other articles were sent home. A ship, on her way from Hispaniola, was captured by him, in the year just mentioned, having on board eighty thousand ducats in gold, six hundred pounds weight—eight ounces to the pound, of pearls and two thousand arrobas, of twenty-five pounds each, of sugar.[1] In the following year, he took possession of seven vessels bound from Cadiz to the Canary islands, with emigrants, but being overhauled off the point of Gando, by vessels sent in pursuit, was compelled to relinquish his prizes.[2]

He is next found apparently meditating an expedition against the Portuguese possessions in Brazil, upon the pretext of discovering other countries in the east, which that nation had not found. The mention of

---

[1] Peter Martyr, *Dec.* v. c. 8. *Epistola* 771 (ed. 1671). In this letter which is dated at Valladolid 19th November, 1522, Martyr writes: "Anno quippe superiore *Florinus quidam Gallus pirata* navim unam ab Hispaniola venientem, auro ad summam octoginta millium dragmarum, unionum vero libris octuncialibus sexcentis & ruborum saccari duobus millibus rapuit."

[2] Don Bartholome Garcia del Castillo in *Noticias de la historia de las islas de Canaria*, by Don Joseph de Viera y Clavijo. (Madrid 1772–84).

this project is positive, and becomes curious and interesting in the history of his life, as it affords the only authentic evidence extant of any suggestion of a voyage of discovery, contemplated by him towards Cathay. The design, if really entertained, appears, however, to have fallen through and to have been abandoned; but it may, nevertheless, have been the foundation of the story of the alleged voyage. It is related by Francisco d' Andrade, in his *Chronicle of John III*, the then reigning king of Portugal. After referring to the death of Magellan, as an event which removed a cause of difference between the crowns of Portugal and Castile, growing out of the famous expedition of that navigator, Andrade thus speaks of the state of affairs between the crowns of France and Portugal.

"At that time, the king was told by some Portuguese, doing business in France, that one João Varezano, a Florentine, offered himself to Francis, to discover other kingdoms in the East, which the Portuguese had not found, and that in the ports of Normandy a fleet was being made ready under the favor of the admirals of the coast, and the dissimulation of Francis, to colonize the land of Santa Cruz, called Brazil, discovered and laid down by the Portuguese in the second voyage to India. This, and the complaints every where made of the injuries inflicted by French corsairs, rendered the early attention of the king necessary.

"Accordingly he sent to France an embassador, João da Silveyra, son of Fernão da Silveyra, who delayed his going no longer than was necessary to get ready. The purpose of his mission was to ask Francis, inasmuch as there never had been war between them, but rather an ancient peace and friendship, that he would give orders throughout his kingdom for the many robberies and injuries, perpetrated at sea on each other by the Portuguese and French, to cease, (which tacitly was a private and not an open war, as in general they were friends); that whatever could be found in his ports taken from the Portuguese, should be restored, as what might be found in the harbors of Portugal, taken from the French, should be forthwith given up, and that to all who should ask justice in this particular it should be rendered immediately and fully. The king then required Francis likewise, to prevent his vessels from making outfits to go to parts of the Portuguese conquest, whither it was not lawful for even Portuguese vessels to sail or the people to traffic.

"João da Silveyra was well received at the court of France; but as respects the specific matters of negotiation in his charge, he was answered every way indefinitely, with reasons more specious than sound which appeared to be given not so much to conclude the affairs upon which he treated as to procrastinate and consume time.

* * * * * * * * * * * *

"João da Silveyra continued to solicit with much urgency the matters in his keeping at the court of France, and received answers respecting them according as the matters which were proposed in Portugal, [the marriage of Carlota, daughter of Francis, with the prince Dom João], gave hopes of advancement. The king said through one Luys Homem that he greatly desired the fostering and increase of ancient friendship. Following upon that in a few days he ordered the vessels in his ports preparing for India to be stopped, stating that he would arrange this in such a way that the king should be satisfied. Measures were adopted for the restoration of all property that was known to have been taken from the king or his vessels, and expectations were entertained of an order making such provision throughout as should put a stop to all the robberies and the evils arising from them. Since this had been the principal object for which the embassador had been sent to France, it appeared to the king of Portugal, that it would be for his service that he should order the return of João da Silveyra, and that the licentiate Pedro Gomez Feixeira with Master Diego de Gevoeya, (to whom he likewise wrote of this matter) should demand justice respecting certain matters of his property and assist such of his vessels as were seeking it. But before the order for the return of Silveyra had left this court, information was received by one Jacome Monteyro (who by authority of the king of France sought the restitution of property) that Francis had issued new orders, commanding the general sequestration of all the property of the king of Portugal and of his people, the embargo of all his vessels to be found in the ports of France, without the declaration of any new cause, or the statement of any reason for this order, the opposite of what had before been promulgated. The king in consequence, directed João da Silveyra to take truthful information of the particulars and the reasons for this proceeding and commanded his presence before the council, to make them known.

"Following this, hostilities having been declared between the kingdoms and seignories of the emperor and the king of France, they waging cruel strife by land and sea, the French with an armament afloat took a Spanish ship with gold, belonging to the emperor, within the limits of the Portuguese coast, besides much property of individuals, regardless of where she had been found, so little attentive were they in those times, to Portugal and Portuguese; seized her by force as belonging to their enemies, and carried her off, as good prize of war. Pedro Batelho was sailing the while, giving protection to the coast of Portugal, by the royal order, according to the ancient custom of this kingdom, held always to be useful and necessary, the value of which became evident from what occurred afterwards, when it fell into disuse.

"The captain coming out one morning with his fleet, near those who were carrying off the Spanish ship, he obliged them by force to take in sail, as they hesitated to obey for some time, until he informed himself of what had passed. Discovering that there were some doubts and that deliberation would be necessary to do justice, he brought all before him to the port of Lisbon, where the prize was sequestrated and they made prisoners, and the case, by order of the king, was sent to the *Casa da Supplicaçam* where sentence was pronounced the following year. This news, which was directly known in France, made great change in the order of affairs with Portugal, and produced the state they were afterwards in, during the following nine consecutive years that João da Silveyra was there, in which time, he accomplished nothing he had in hand, except to *embargo the voyage of the Florentine*, of which mention is made before, and of some few vessels of corsairs which was but sheer justice to us." [1]

The time when these preparations were being made by Verrazzano, is more definitely fixed by a despatch of Silveira to the king, from Paris on the 25th of April 1523, in which he states that "Verazano" had not yet left for Cathay.[2] It is highly probable, therefore,

---

[1] *Cronica de muyto alto, e muyto poderoso rey destes reynos de Portugal Dom João o* III *deste nome.* By Francisco d' Andrade. Part I, c. 13 and 14. (Lisbon 1613.)

[2] Santarem gives the date of this despatch as of the 23d of April 1522, *Quadro Elementar*, tom. III, sec. XVI, p. 165. But the letter of Silveira will be found in full in the Appendix (I.) from the Portuguese archives. Santarem

that this whole story of an intended voyage of discovery was proposed for the purpose of concealing the real object of the preparations which were going on in Normandy, of seizing the treasure which had been sent from Mexico, by Cortes to the emperor, of the successful accomplishment of which we have now to speak.

In November, 1522, a vessel arrived in Spain which had been sent from Mexico, by the conquistador with the emperor's share of the tribute money collected in that country, in the special charge of Alonzo Davila and Antonio Quiñones, with other articles of value. Fearing capture by the French corsairs, this vessel had sailed by the way of the Azores, and leaving the treasure, with its custodians, at the island of Santa Maria, proceeded on without it, in order that a proper force might be sent to that island to bring it safely to Spain. Juan Ribera, the secretary of Cortes, came in the ship to Spain. These facts appear to have become notorious immediately. Peter Martyr mentions them in his letter of the 17th of November 1522, and in the fifth of his decades, written while the treasure was still at Santa Maria, speaks of the French having knowledge of its being left there. "I know not," he says, "in reference to the ships sent there for it, what flying report there is that the French pirates have understood of those ships, God grant them good successe."[1] Three caravels were despatched from Seville

---

is evidently mistaken as to the year, inasmuch as the news of Magellan's death, to which Andrade refers as a prior event, did not reach Spain until September 1522 and Silveira's appointment as embassador was after that news was received.

[1] *Dec.* v. c. 10. (Lok's trans.)

to Santa Maria, under the command of Captain Domingo Alonzo, arriving there on the 15th of May 1523. Davila and Quiñones immediately embarked in them, with the treasure, sailing directly to Spain. Meanwhile, Verrazzano proceeded with six vessels towards Cape St. Vincent, for the purpose of intercepting them, which he succeeded in doing, within ten leagues of that cape. After a sharp encounter, in which Quiñones was killed, he captured two of them, in one of which Davila was taken with the gold, and the other most valuable articles. The third caravel escaped, and arrived in Spain, with a tiger and various articles of rich manufacture, which had belonged to Montezuma. Verrazzano took his prizes into Rochelle. The value of the treasure and articles taken was estimated at more than six hundred thousand ducats, or one million and a half of dollars.[1]

These facts at least establish that João Verazano mentioned by the Portuguse, Andrade and Silveira, was the same person who made the capture of the treasure ships; for it is not to be supposed that two different Florentines of the name of Giovanni, were in command of French fleets, at the same time, belonging to the ports of Normandy alone; and consequently that Verrazzano, our navigator, and Juan Florin the corsair were one. But how far the seizure of the treasure ships was, as before suggested, the original pur-

---

[1] Peter Martyr, *Dec.* v. c. 8. *Epist.* 771, Nov. 19, 1522, and 779, June, 11, 1523 (ed. 1670). Herrera, *Dec.* III. lib. IV. c. 20. Letter of Davila to the emperor from Rochelle, June 17, 1523, in the archives at Seville, now first published in the Appendix (IV), Martyr says there were two ships, the larger of which only, containing the treasure fell into the hands of John Florin, the French pirate, and the other escaped; but Davila must be right.

pose of the fleet can only be inferred from the circumstances, and is important only in connection with the *design* of a voyage of discovery. Between the time of the arrival of Ribera with the information that the treasure had been left at the Azores, and the sending of the caravels to bring it to Spain, nearly six months elapsed. Taking the dates, which are established by the official documents now produced, of the fitting out of the fleet in Normandy by Verrazzano and the actual capture of the two caravels, it is easy to see that the real purpose of those preparations from the first, might have been to effect the capture of the treasure. The transmission of the news to Portugal of an intended voyage to Brazil and the sending of instructions to the embassador at[1] the French court could all have taken place after the detention of the treasure at Santa Maria became known in France and the fitting out of the vessels for its capture had begun to be made. It is stated by Andrade that it was at a port in Normandy where the vessels were being made ready; and it is to be presumed, from the connection of Verrazzano with Jean Ango, as shown subsequently by the agreement with Chabot for a like purpose, that it was from Dieppe, and probably at the expense of that rich merchant, who we are told was enabled to entertain his sovereign with princely magnificence and to embargo the port of Lisbon, with a fleet of his own,[2] that they sailed on this occasion.

Verrazzano is certainly found at Rochelle on the 16th of June, 1523, two months after the despatch of Silveira

---

[1] According to the letter of Silveira, he was at Poissy on Christmas, and Andrade was therefore, probably in error in stating that he had his instructions in regard to *Varezano* before he left Portugal.

[2] *Mem. Chron. de Dieppe.* I. 106–111.

was written, with his prizes captured on a different expedition from that mentioned by the ambassador. It is evident, therefore, that the project of a voyage of discovery to Cathay, if ever seriously entertained, had at that time been abandoned; as may also be inferred from the statement of Andrade, that Silveira, in the nine years he was at the court of France, succeeded only in embargoing the voyage of the Florentine, and accomplishing some minor matters.[1]

But the question of any such voyage of discovery having been made at the time claimed in the Verrazzano letter is effectually set at rest by the fact that Verrazzano was then actually engaged in a corsairial enterprise elsewhere. Peter Martyr, in an epistle written on the 3d of August 1524, less than a month after the alleged return of Verrazzano to Dieppe from his voyage of discovery, wrote from Valladolid that " a courier of the king of Portugal had arrived (with word) that *Florin, the French pirate*, had captured a ship of his king on her way from the Indies, with a cargo valued at one hundred and eighty thousand ducats."[2] It is impossible for Verrazzano to have been on the coast of North America, or on his return from Newfoundland to France, and at the same time to have taken a ship on her way from the Indies to Portugal, coming as she must have done, by the Cape of Good Hope.

The defeat of Francis I at the battle of Pavia and his capture and detention in Spain during the year

---

[1] The document accompanying the letter of Davila in the archives, describes Juan Florin as of Dieppe, and thus fixes the seat of his operations in Normandy. See Appendix, (IV. 2.)

[2] *Epist.* 800 (ed. 1670).

1525, seem to have suspended the depredations upon the seas by the French, and nothing more occurs relating to Verrazzano, until after the release of the king, in the following year, and then in an adventure which seems to have cost him his life, unless his probable appearance in England as mentioned by Hakluyt, to which reference has already been made, be an exception. Allusion has also been made several times to an agreement between Chabot, admiral of France, and others, including Verrazzano, which now assumes particular importance. It is the only document yet produced in France, relating to him, and is of recent discovery.[1] By this agreement it was stipulated that Chabot, as admiral of France, should furnish two galleons, Jean Ango one ship, and Verrazzano two pilots besides himself, and that the three persons here named should with Guillaume Preudhomme, general of Normandy, Pierre Despinolles and Jacques Boursier, in different specified amounts each, make up the sum of twenty thousand pounds in Tours currency for the expenses, on joint account, of a voyage to the Indies for spices,— the admiral and Ango, however, to have one-fourth of all the merchandise returned, for the use of the vessels, and Verrazzano to have one-sixth of the remaining three-fourths, for his compensation and that of his two pilots. The contract contained another provision, that if any booty should be taken on the sea from the Moors, or other enemies of the faith and the king, the admiral should first take a tenth of it and the remainder should be divided as stipulated in regard to

---

[1] Margry, *Les Navigations Françaises*, p. 194. (Paris, 167.) See Appendix (II.)

the merchandise, except such part as should, upon advisement, be given to the crew. The admiral was to have letters patent expedited from the king for permission to make the voyage. This paper has no date, but as it was made by Chabot, in his official capacity, as admiral of France, it could not have been earlier than March 1526, when, as we have seen, he was so created. It belongs, therefore, either to that or the following year, judging from the fatal consequences which happened to Verrazzano in the latter.

Although a voyage from France to the Indies for spices was not an improbable venture at that time, inasmuch as one was actually made from Dieppe, two years afterwards, by Jean Parmentier in the service of Ango, there is every reason to believe that such was not the real object of the parties to this agreement. One of the stipulations between them was for a division of booty, showing an intention to make captures on the sea. Who were the enemies of the king from whom it was to be taken is not stated. By the treaty of Madrid, in January 1526, peace existed between France and Spain, and any expedition from one of them against the commerce of the other, was clearly piratical. Neither did war exist at this time, between France and Portugal. Yet it appears that both the Spaniards and the Portuguese, were searching for Verrazzano at the time, when the former succeeded in capturing him, in September or October 1527. He had, therefore, not sailed to the Indies and must have made himself obnoxious to those nations, by fresh depredations upon their vessels. Bernal Diaz, who gives an account of his capture and execution, states that he was actually so engaged.¹ It appears from the letters of the judge who superintended his execution that he was then encountered by six Biscayan galleons and ships, and after battle, captured and taken by them to Cadiz, with his crew, consisting of one hundred and twenty or thirty persons, besides several gentlemen adventurers. Verrazzano offered his captors thirty thousand ducats to be released, but in vain. He was sent under guard with the adventurers to Madrid, but was overtaken on the way at Colmenar near Puerto del Pico, villages between Salamanca and Toledo,² by the judge of Cadiz with an order made by the emperor at Lerma on the 13th of October 1527, by virtue of which he was there put to death in November of that year. Such was the termination of the career of this bold man, which was long ago substantially told by Bernal Diaz and Barcia, but so loosely in regard to dates, as to have created doubts as to their correctness, but which is established by the documents existing in the archives at Simancas, now brought to light.³

---

¹ *Historia verdadera*, fol. 164.

² Blaeu, *Utriusque Castiliæ nova descriptio*. Martiniere, *Dictionaire Géographique, sub* Colmenar *et* Pico.

³ See the letter of the judge of Cadiz, in the Appendix (v.ɪ.) Barcia, in his Chronological Essay, mentions the capture and execution of Juan the Florentine as a pirate under the year 1524. He does not state that they took place in that year, but refers to them in connection with the discoveries alleged to have been made in that year by Verrazzano, whom he identifies as the corsair. It has been supposed, consequently, that he meant that year as the time of Verrazzano's death; and hence, inasmuch as Verrazzano was known to have been alive after that year, that the whole story was an error. The letters of Juan de Giles, the resident judge of Cadiz, appended to this memoir, enable us to fix the date of his execution, for although not dated themselves, they contain a reference to the date of the cedule, ordering the execution, by which it can be determined. Giles mentions that this cedule was dated at *Lerma, on the* 13*th of last month*, showing that it was made there on the 13th of some month. According to the Itinerary of Charles V, kept by his private secretary, Vandernesse, containing

THE LIFE AND DEATH OF VERRAZZANO. 149

And thus finally the testimony, upon which the tale of discovery was credited and proclaimed to the world, is contradicted and disproved. The statement that Verrazzano and a member of his crew were killed and then feasted upon by the inhabitants of the coast which he had visited a second time, has no support or confirmation in the history of that rude and uncivilized people; for, however savage and cruel they were towards their enemies, or, under provocation, towards strangers, no authenticated instance of their canibalism has ever been produced; but on the contrary the testimony of the best authorities, is that they were guiltless of any such horrid practice. Yet that statement was a part of the information which Ramusio received and communicated to his readers at the same time with the Verrazzano letter; and constituted a part of the evidence upon which he relied. How utterly false it was is shown by the agreement with Chabot and the capture and execution of Verrazzano by the Spaniards. It is now seen how the credulity of the historian was imposed upon, and he was led by actual

---

an account of the emperor's journeys from the year 1519 to 1551, Charles went to Lerma, a small town in Old Castile, for the first time on the 9th of May, 1524, and returned thence to Burgos on the 12th of that month, going to Lerma again on the 21st of July of that year and leaving it on the 24th for Vallidesole. He was not there afterwards, until the 12th of October, 1527, where he remained until the 17th of that month when he went to Burgos. He went to Lerma again on the 20th of February 1528, and remained there for two days only. These are all the occasions of his presence at Lerma during the whole period of the Itinerary. These dates prove that the only possible occasion for issuing the order of execution was the 13th of October 1527. The prisoners left under guard, on the 15th of that month for Madrid, and the letter apprising the emperor that the order had been executed upon Verrazzano, must have been written in November, the month following.

The Itinerary will be found in the *Correspondence of the Emperor Charles V*, by William Bradford, London, 1850.

misrepresentations to adopt a narrative which has no foundation in truth, and whose inconsistencies and incongruities he vainly sought to reconcile, but which, for three centuries, sanctioned by his authority alone, has been received as authentic and true; until at length, by the exposure of its original character, and the circumstances of its publication by him, with the production of undoubted evidence from the records of the time, it is proven to be a deliberate fraud.

This completes our purpose. The question, however, still presents itself, what was the motive for this gross deception? The answer is suggested by the fact that all the evidence produced in favor of the story is traceable to Florence, the birthplace of Verrazzano. Ramusio obtained the Verrazzano letter there,— the only one, he says, not astray in consequence of its unfortunate troubles. The letter of Carli, enclosing that of Verrazzano, is professedly written by a Florentine to his father in that city. The map of Hieronimo de Verrazano bears the impress of the family. The discourse of the French captain of Dieppe appears to have been sent originally to Florence, whence it was procured by Ramusio. Even the globe of Euphrosynus Ulpius, a name otherwise unknown, is represented to have been constructed for Marcellus, who had been archbishop of Florence. They are all the testimony of Florence in her own behalf. The cities of Italy which had grown in wealth and importance during the fifteenth century, by means of an enterprising and valuable commerce, produced and nurtured a race of skillful seamen, among whom were the most distinguished of the first discoverers of the new world, in the persons of Columbus, Vespucci and the Cabots; but those cities contributed nothing more to the discoveries which thus were achieved, than to give these men birth and education. The glory of promoting and successfully accomplishing those results belonged to other nations, which had the wisdom and fortune to secure the services of these navigators. The cities shone, however, with the lustre reflected from having reared and instructed them to the work they so wonderfully performed. Although enjoying a common nationality, these municipalities belonged to independent republics and were in a measure rivals of each other. Florence emulated Genoa. She truly boasted that Vespucci, born and raised on her soil, was the first to reach the main land and thus to have his name applied to the whole continent, "America quasi Americi terra;" while Genoa justly claimed for her son, that the discovery of all America was to be regarded as assured from the moment that Columbus landed on the little sandy island of Guanahana, on the 12th of October 1492.[1] But Florence enjoys in addition the unenviable distinction of having sought to advance the pretensions of Vespucci by fictitious letters, purporting to be signed with his name.[2] That this spirit of civic pride in that same community may have actuated the fabrication of the Verrazzano letter is not improbable; but in justice to the memory of Verrazzano it must be added, there is no reason to believe that he was in any way accessory to the imposture.

---

[1] Humboldt, *Examen Critique*, IV, 37.
[2] Varnhagen, *Amerigo Vespucci, son caractére, ses ecrits (méme les moins authentiques) &c.*, p. 67, *et seq.* (Lima, 1865).

APPENDIX.

APPENDIX.

I.

LETTERA DI FERNANDO CARLI A SUO PADRE.

From the Archivo Storico Italiano. Appendice Tomo IX. 53-5. Firenze 1853.

Al nome di Dio

a dì 4 Agosto 1524.

" Onorando padre.— Considerando che quando fui in la armata di Barbaria alle Gierbe vi furono grate le nuove advisatevi giornalmente per lo illustre sig. Don Ugo di Moncada, capitano generale della Cesarea Maestà in quelle barbare parti, seguite certando (1) con li Mori di detta isola; per la quale mostrasi haver fatto piacere a molti nostri padroni ed amici, e con quelli della conseguita vittoria congratulatovi: pertanto, essendo nuovamente qui nuova della giunta del capitano Giovanni da Verrazzano nostro fiorentino allo porto di Diepa in Normandia con sua nave Delfina, con la quale si partì dalle insule Canarie fino di Gennaio passato, per andare in busca di terre nuove per questa serenissima corona di Francia, in che mostrò coraggio troppo nobile e grande a mettersi a tanto incognito viaggio con una sola nave che appena è una caravella di tonelli   (2), solo con 50 uomini, con intenzione di, giusta sua possa, discoprire il Cataio, tenendo cammino per altri climati di quelli usano li Portughesi in lo discoprire di verso la parte di

---

(1) Combattendo (*Nota dell'edizione Romana*).
(2) L'amanuense ha lasciato il numero delle tonnellate di cui era capace la nave (*Nota come sopra*).

Calicut, ma andando verso coro e settentrione *omnino* tenendo, che ancora (1) Tolomeo ed Aristotile ed altri cosmografi descrivano verso tali climati non trovarsi terra, di trovarvene a ogni modo; e cosi gli ha Dio concesso, come distintamente descrive per una sua lettera a questa S. M.; della quale in questa ne è una copia. E per mancargli le vettovaglie, dopo molti mesi giunto navigando, assegna essergli stato forza tornar da quello in questo emisperio, e in sette mesi suto in viaggio mostrare grandissimo ed accelerato cammino, aver fatto cosa miranda e massima a chi intende la marinera del mondo. Della quale al cominciamento di detto suo viaggio si fece male iuditio (2), e molti pensorno che non più nè di lui nè del vascello si avesse nuova, ma che si dovesse perdere da quella banda della Norvegia per il grande diaccio che è per quello oceano settentrionale: ma come disse quel Moro, lo Dio grande, per darci ogni giorno più notizie di sua infinita possanza e mostrarci di quanto sia admirabile questa mundiale machina, gli ha discoperto una latitudine di terra, come intenderete, di tanta grandezza che, secondo le buone ragioni e gradi, per latitudine (et) altezza, assegna e mostra più grande che l'Europa, Africa e parte di Asia: *ergo mundus novus:* e questo senza lo che (3) hanno discoperto in più anni gli Spani per l'occidente, che appena è un anno tornò Ferrando Magaghiana, quale discoperse grande paese con una nave meno delle cinque (4) a discoprire. Donde addusse garofani molto più eccellenti delli soliti; e le altre sue navi in 5 anni mai nuova ci è trapelata. Stimansi perse. Quello (5) che questo nostro capitano abbia condotto non dice per questa sua lettera, salvo uno uomo giovanetto preso di quelli paesi; ma stimansi che abbia portato mostra di oro, poichè da quelle bande non lo stimano, e di droghe e di altri liquori aromatici, per conferire qua con molti mercatanti di poi

---

(1) Ancorchè.
(2) L'ediz. romana ha *indizio*, ma crediamo per errore di stampa.
(3) Quello che (*Nota come sopra*).
(4) Forse venne qui omesso *ite* o simile; e sembra accennarsi al naufragio di una di quelle cinque navi.
(5) Nella romana si legge: "stimansi per sè quello ec."; ma ci sembra che il senso giustifichi abbastanza la nostra correzione.

che sarà stato alla presenza della Serenissima Maestà. E a questa ora doverrà esservi, e di qua trasferirsi in breve, perchè è molto desiato, per ragionare seco; tanto più che troverà qui la Maestà del Re nostro sire, che fra tre o quattro giorni vi si attende: e speriamo che S. M. lo rimetta di mezza dozzina di buoni vascelli, e che tornerà al viaggio. E se Francesco Carli nostro ci fosse tornato dal Cairo, advisate che alla ventura vorrà andare seco a detto viaggio, e credo si conoschino al Cairo dove è stato più anni; e non solo in Egitto ed Soria, ma quasi per tutto il cognito mondo; e di qua mediante sua virtù è stimato un altro Amerigo Vespucci, un altro Ferrando Magaghiana, e davantaggio; e speriamo che rimontandosi delle altre buone navi e vascelli ben conditi e vettovagliati come si richiede, abbia ad iscoprire qualche profittoso traffico e fatto; e farà, prestandogli nostro Signore Dio vita, onore alla nostra patria da acquistarne immortale fama e memoria. E Alderotto Brunelleschi che partì con lui, e per fortuna tornando indietro non volse più seguire, come di costà lo intende, sarà malcontento. Nè altro per ora mi occorre, perchè per altre vi ho avvisato il bisogno. A voi di continuo mi raccomando, pregandovi ne facciate parte agli amici nostri, non dimenticando Pierfrancesco Dagaghiano (1), che per essere persona perita, tengo che ne prenderà grande passatempo; ed a lui mi raccomanderete. Simile al Rustichi, al quale non dispiacerà se si diletta, come suole, intendere cose di cosmografia. Che Dio tutti di male vi guardi.

Vostro figliuolo
FERNANDO CARLI in Lione.

---

(1) Forse, da Gagliano.

II.

AGREEMENT OF PHILIPPE CHABOT, ADMIRAL OF FRANCE, WITH CERTAIN ADVENTURERS INCLUDING VERRAZZANO.

From the Fontette Collection, xxi, 770, fol. 60, in the Bibliothèque Nationale in Paris.
* First printed by M. Margry, and here corrected according to the MS.

Nous, Philippe Chabot, baron d'Apremont, chevalier de l'ordre du Roi, son gouverneur et lieutenant general de Bourgoingne, admiral de France et de Bretaine.

Avons ce jourdhuy deliberé que, pour le bien, prouffict et utilité de la chose publicque du royaulme de France, mettre sur deux de nos gallyons estant de present au Havre de Grâce avec une nef appartenant à Jehan Ango, de Dieppe, du port soixantedix tonneaulx ou environ, por iceulx troys veseaulx, esquipper, vitailler et convinyr, pour faire le voiaige des espiceryes aux Indies.— Dont pour icelluy voiage faire avons accordé avec les personnes cidessoubz nommés et signez en la manière qui ensuict pour fournyr lesd. trois navyres de marchandises, victailles et avance de compaignons ainsi qu'il sera requis et nécessaire.

Et pour ce faire avons conclud et deliberé, avec iceulx, mectre et employer jusques à la somme de vingt mil livres tour, c'est assavoir, pour nous Admiral quatre mille livres tour, maistre Guillaume Preudhomme, général de Normandye, deux mil livres tour; Pierre Despinolles, mil livres tour; Jehan Ango, deux mil livres tour; Jacques Boursier, pareille somme de deux mil livres tournoys, messire Jehan de Varesam, principalle pilote, semblable somme de deux mil livres tournoys.

Lesd. parties revenans ensemble à la somme de vingt mil livres tournoys. Por icelle employer aux vitailles, marchandises et avance, loyèr de compagnons. Et nous Amyral et Ango prometons bailler lesd. gallyons et nef, bien et deuement radoubées et accoustrées, comme il appartient à faire led voyaige, tant de calfadages, cables, ancres, doubles appareilz, tous cordages, artilleryes, pouldres, boullets, et tout ce qui est requiz à telz navires pour faire ung tel et si long voiaige que cestuy et rendre iceulx gallyons et nefs prestz, et apareillez à faire led. voiaige dedans deux moys de ce jourduy Par ainsy que nous Admiral et Ango, prenderons au retour dud. voiaige, poùr le fret et noleage desd. gallyons et nef, le cart de toutes les marchandises qui reviendront et seront rapportes par iceulx, sans aucune chose payer.

Et pour le loyer dud¹·t messire Jehan pillote, lequel s'est submis et obligé de fournyr deux pillotes bons et suffisans pour conduire les deux aultres navires, prendra pr son dict loyer et de ses deux pillotes, le sixiesme de tout se qui reviendra de marchandises, led. cart por nolliage, les frais et mises des marchandises et loyers des cōpaignons en préalable prins et levés avant que prendre led. sixiesme.

Et se, par cas de fortune, aucuns d'iceulx gallyons ou nef feussent pdus aud. voiaige, ou que l'ung p quelque incōvenient et les deux aultres feissent leur voiaige, la marchandise qui reviendroit se p̃teroit comme dessus et y ptiroit led. navire qui n'ayroit esté audict voyage et les marchans, chacun au marc la livre, car tout va a commun profit.

Et se aucun butin se faict à la mer sur les Mores, ou aultres ennemys de la Foy et du Roy; monseigneur l'Amyral prendera en prealable sur icelluy butin son xme, et le reste qui revenderoit dud. butin se ptira comme l'autre marchandise, sauf quelque portion d'icelluy butin, que l ong baillera aux cōpagnons ainsi qu'il sera avisé.

Et fera mond. sr Lamyral expedier lētres du Roy en patent pour avoir licence et congé de faire led. voiaige, et que aucun empeschement ne leur sera fet ou donné par aucune nation des aliez, amys ou cōfenderez du Roy nōre d sr.

Pour le voiage de messire Joan.

[Translation.]

We, Philippe Chabot, Baron d'Apremont, Knight of the Ordre du Roi, his Governor and Lieutenant-general of Burgundy, Admiral of France and of Brittany,

Have this day determined for the good, advantage, and utility of the public affairs of the Kingdom of France, to put two of our galleons, at present at Havre de Grace, with one ship belonging to Jehan Ango of Dieppe, of seventy tons burden, or thereabouts, to equip, victual and fit these three vessels, to make the voyage for spices to the Indies. To make the aforesaid voyage, we have agreed with the persons hereinafter named and signed, in the manner following, to furnish the said three vessels with goods, victuals, and advance money for the crew, as shall be requisite and necessary.

And to do this we have concluded and determined with the aforesaid, to put and employ as large a sum as twenty thousand pounds, Tours currency, that is to say, for ourself, Admiral, four thousand pounds, Tours; Master Guillaume Preudhomme, General of Normandy, two thousand pounds, Tours; Pierre Despinolles, one thousand pounds, Tours; Jehan Ango, two thousand pounds, Tours; Jacques Boursier, an equal sum of two thousand pounds, Tours; Messire Jehan de Varesam, Chief pilot, a like sum of two thousand pounds, Tours.

The said parts together amounting to the said sum of 20,000 pounds, Tours,[1] to be employed for provisions, merchandise, and advance money to hire the crew. And we, Admiral and Ango, promise to deliver the said galleons and ship well and properly refitted and accoutred, as befits to make the said voyage, as well as caulkings, cables, anchors, duplicate furniture, all cordage, artillery, powder, shot, and all that is required by such vessels, to make such a long voyage as this; and to have these gal-

---

[1] The sums here named do not make twenty thousand pounds.— TRANSLATOR.

leons and ship ready and prepared to make the said voyage within two months from this day. Also, that we, Admiral and Ango, will take, on the return from the said voyage, for the freight and freighting of the said galleons and ship, the fourth part of all the merchandise which shall return and shall be brought back by the aforesaid, without any cost.

And for the hire of the said pilot, Messire Jehan, who has agreed and bound himself to provide two good and competent pilots to steer the other two vessels, he shall take for his hire and that of his two pilots, the sixth of all the goods which shall be brought back; the said fourth for freightage, expenses and disposing of the goods, and the wages of the crew, being previously taken and levied, before taking the said sixth.

And if, in case of accident, any of those galleons or ship should be lost on the said voyage, or if one by any mischance does not, and the other two do make their voyage, the merchandise which should be brought back, would be divided as above, and the said vessel which might not have been on the said voyage shall share, and the merchants each one a mark to the pound, for all goes to the common profit.

And if any booty be taken at sea, from the Moors or others enemies of the Faith and the King, my Lord; the Admiral, shall take previously, of the aforesaid booty, his tenth; and the balance which would accrue from the said booty, shall be divided like the other goods, except some portion of that booty, which shall be given to the crew as shall be advised.

And my aforesaid Admiral shall have letters-patent from the king expedited, in order to have permission and leave to make the said voyage; and no obstruction shall be made or given to these letters, by any allies, friend, or confederate of the king, our said Lord.

For the voyage of Sir Joan.

III.

Letter of Joao da Silveira, the Portuguese Ambassador in France, to King Dom João III.

Translated from the original at Lisbon, in *Archivo de Torre de Tombo, Corp. Chron. Part I. Ma.* 29. *Doc.* 54.

Sire:

I received a letter from Your Highness on the 19th of this month, through João Francisco, wherein I am directed what is to be done respecting the galleon and caravel, taken at the deira Islands,[1] by the galleys of France. As soon as I received the instruction, which was about the beginning of Christmas, I spoke on the subject in a manner befitting the nature of the case. At once they were released,—the caravel with her artillery and the brocades and silks.[2] By this time they must have arrived at Lisbon. As respects the merchandise, I had the promise that if it was found to be the property of Your Highness or of your subjects it should not be sold. After a few days, discovering that it belonged to João Francisco, an ample order was given to his agents for its entire restitution, which orders set forth that as he lives in the kingdoms of Your Highness, and there is an old friendship existing with the King of France which he was no less desirous of preserving, in this he would favor that king. After this order was promulgated another came from the chief official, in consequence of which nothing was delivered, and the goods moreover were sold. From that time to the present, nothing has been accomplished. I will strive the best I can for despatch, in the manner that Your Highness points out, and will give account of what I do.

---

[1] Probably Madeira Islands. Translator.

[2] That is to say, the hangings, tapestry, and awnings of the vessel. Translator.

When the matter of the galleon occurred, the Licentiate Pero Gomez had already embarked at Anaflor. I advised the Doctor, Maestro Diogo, who was about going to Reuão[1] that he ought not to leave before writing, and to give Your Highness a statement of the facts in that regard; as he at once wrote that he would do so, I have said nothing further in my letters.

By what I hear, Maestro João Verazano, who is going on the discovery of Cathay, has not left up to this date, for want of opportunity and because of differences, I understand, between himself and men; and on this topic, though knowing nothing positively, I have written my doubts in accompanying letters. I shall continue to doubt unless he take his departure.

The Doctor Maestro Diogo de Gouvea is now going to Ruão[1] where he is going to find out everything with the greatest exactness possible, and, as I have requested, report at great length. May our Lord prolong the life of Your Highness many days and prosper the royal estate.

From Poessi the xxv of April 1523.

João da Silveira.

---

[1] i. e. Rouen. Translator.

IV.

1. Letter of Alonso Davila to the Emperor Charles V, relating to the Capture of the Treasure sent from Mexico by Cortes.

<small>Translated from the original in the Archivo de Indias at Seville.</small>

Very high and very powerful Catholic Lord King:

Captain Domingo Alonso, who was commander of the three caravels that sailed as guard on the coast of Andalusia, gave a cedula to Antonio Quiñones and myself at the Island of Azores, in which Your Majesty was pleased to state to us that, from the news of our fear of the French who were said to run the coast, we had remained at the island of Santa Maria until your Highness should direct what might be for the royal service, in so doing we had acted well; that to secure the gold and articles we had brought, the three caravels were sent to us under that captain; and we were enjoined to embark in them at once and come with every thing to the city of Seville, to the House of Contratacion, and the officers who by the royal command reside there, for which favor we kiss your feet and hands.

The caravels arrived the xvth of May, and directly in fulfilment of the order we embarked, sailing for the Portuguese coast, which the pilots deemed the safer course, and coming within ten leagues of Cape St. Vincent, six armed French ships ran out upon us. We fought them from two caravels, until we were overpowered, when everything eminently valuable on the way to Your Majesty was lost; the other caravel not being disposed to fight escaped to carry the news; and but for that perhaps the captain might better have staid with his additional force to aid our defence than to carry back such tidings. Quiñones died, and I am a prisoner at Rochelle in France.

I should desire to come, would they but let me, to kiss your royal feet, and give a complete history of all; for I lost everything I possessed in the service of Your Majesty, and have wished that my life had been as well. I entreat that privileges be granted to the residents and inhabitants of New Spain and that you will consider services to have been rendered, since that people have loyally done their duty to this moment, and will ever do as true vassals.

I beseech that Your Majesty be pleased to order good protection placed on the coast of Andalusia for the ships coming from the Indies; for now all the French, flushed as they are, desire to take positions whence they may commit mischief. Let it be an armament that can act offensively, and which will not flee, but seek out the enemy.

I entreat, prisoner and lost as I am, yet desiring still to die in the royal service, that Your Highness will so favor me, that if any ship should be sent to New Spain, an order be directed to Hernando Cortes, requiring that the Indians I have there deposited in the name of Your Majesty be not taken, but that they be bestowed on me for the period that is your pleasure.

Our Lord augment the imperial state of Your Royal Majesty to the extent your royal person may require.

From Rochela of France, the xvith day of June of M. d. xxiij years.

Of Y. C. Ca. Ma. the loyal vassal who kisses your very royal feet and hands.

Alonso Davila.

2. Statement Concerning the French Vessels of War which Cruise the Sea of Spain.

Translated from the original in the *Archivo de Indias* at Seville, in the same hand, says Dr. D. Francisco Xuarez, the ancient *archivero*, as the letter of Alonso Davila addressed from Rochelle to the emperor. The hand writing is most difficult to make out. The amounts marked cii may intend ccc, and ci two cc.

The French vessels of war which cruise the sea of Spain as far as Andalusia, of which Jn. Florin *le Diepa* is captain.

First, a large ship cii. tons, in which are cii men — the half soldiers, and the other half sailors; carries xx pieces of artillery of brass, besides others of iron, with munitions and victuals in large quantity.

Another vessel, built in Vizcaya, captured by the French of cɪ tons.

Another vessel of cɪ tons, made in Britany.

Five galleons — the largest of lxx tons, another of lx, another of l, another of xl, made in Vizcaya, another of xl, which are also provided with cc men of war, being of the French soldiers who were in Tuenteravia. They have besides full supply of men & of artillery, munition and victuals for one year; and, it is said, that this armada goes direct to Andalusia, to run that coast and take what may come from the Indias; for this is the same armada that last year took the cxxm ducats that were coming, consequently, it is necessary that His Majesty should have an armada in Andalusia to go to meet this one of France, and not suffer it to do mischief.

V.

1. LETTER FROM THE JUDGE OF CADIZ TO CHARLES V, GIVING THE NAMES OF THE PRINCIPAL PERSONS CAPTURED WITH JUAN FLORIN, AND OF HIS DEATH.

Translated from the original, in the Archivo general in Simancos. Estado: Legajo 13, fol. 346.

Sacred Caesarean Catholic Majesty.

The Licentiate Juan de Giles your Resident Judge in the City of Cadiz reports what has been done in the taking of Juan Florin, a French corsair, and others, made prisoners with him. Before receiving a cedula signed by Your Majesty at Lerma, the thirteenth of last month, knowing that there were some differences of opinion among those making the capture, I labored, and with success, to induce them to bring Juan Florin, Monsr. de la Sala, Monsr Juan de Mensieris, Michel and a page of Juan Florin before Your Majesty, to avoid certain difficulties that were impending. This was done by Bartolome del Alamo, high-sheriff of said City, with six persons, one from each ship engaged in the capture. These took their departure on the 15th of last month, carrying their prisoners to court; and by virtue of the cedula of Your Majesty, I caused the delivery to me of the remaining French to be kept securely as Your Highness required. One hundred and twenty or one hundred and thirty of them were given up, and were in custody when a certain dispatch came to hand from your Counsel on the twenty seventh of last month. In obedience thereto, I ordered the chief Alcalde of said city to proceed against these in my power, agreeably to what was commanded me by your Counsel; and with the utmost speed I came on in pursuit of Juan Florin to Colmenar de Arenas where were executed on his person the laws of your kingdom. Mon^{sr}

de Mensieris, Michel and Gile I condemned perpetually to the galleys; and because the High Sheriff and the Vizcaynos left Monsr de la Sale at the point of death with Juan Lopez de Çumaya, a Vizcaino, who go by another road, I send the High Sheriff for him while I return to Cadiz to make provision for things not done in a manner best befitting the royal service.

In pursuance of your Majesty's order I take especial care that no person ransom or conceal himself. Those of consideration, captured with Juan Florin are Monsr de la Sala, doctor indiscretis, a native of Paris, Monsr Juan de Mensieris, a native of Turenne, son of Martin Mensieris, who has an income of two hundred ducats, Monsr de Londo, a native of Lombardy, son of a gentleman, a Baron, native of Venice, Monsr de Lane, second son of Monsr de Lane, Monsr Vipar, a native of Drumar, son of Monsr Vipar, who is rich, and Monsr Fasan.

S. C. C. M. I kiss the sacred feet of Your Majesty.

LICENCIADO GILES.

2. LETTER OF THE JUDGE OF CADIZ, IN ANSWER TO A ROYAL MISSIVE, STATING BY WHOM JUAN FLORIN WAS CAPTURED, AND HIS EXECUTION.

Translated from the original in the Archivo general in Simancas.
ESTADO : Legajo 13, fol. 345.

Sacred Caesarean Catholic Majesty:

The Licentiate Giles, Resident Judge in the City of Cadiz, in compliance with what your Majesty required by your cedula that it should be stated who captured Juan Florin and his accomplices, answers that Martin Yriçar, Antonio de Çumaya, Juan Martinez de Ariçabalo, Martin Perez de Leabur, Saba de Ysasa, Juan de Galarza, Captains of their galleons and ships, with their people, were those who captured Juan Florin in the manner that they will relate, and brought him to the Bay of Cadiz. I went directly to their galleons, and to my requirement they answered that they would keep him in safety, that they desired all for your service; and this notwithstanding that the said Juan Florin promised them thirty thousand ducats to be released. The captains of the fleet of Portugal who were cruising at sea in quest of him at the same place in which he was taken also offered ten thousand ducats for him that they might take him to their king, and other offers were made, none of which they would accept, but, unitedly, with the sheriff of that city, took him to Your Majesty, like good and loyal servants. And when they arrived at Puerto del Pico, finding Your Majesty had commanded that he and his said accomplices should be given up to me at once, they delivered and I executed the law upon them.

Those captains have sustained much injury and have been at much cost, as I am witness. They arrived with their ships broken, the sails rent, the castles carried away. They had spent much in munition and powder, and for the sustenance of those French before they delivered them to me. When they arrived in the bay they were greatly reduced and hungered, having exhausted their stores by giving to the French. Much would it be for the service of Your Majesty that those Captains should be satisfied for their losses and rewarded which I have promised them, as Your Highness desired by your cedula, that others seeing how they are honored may be encouraged in the royal service. Thus much I entreat that Your Majesty will order done for the loyalty I know those captains bear to your service, and because they are persons by whom you may be much served.

S. C. C. M. I kiss the sacred feet of your Highness.

LICENCIADO GILES.

VI.

The Verrazzano Letter according to the Original Version.

Translated by Dr. J. G. Cogswell, from a copy of the MS. in the Magliabechian library in Florence, and printed in the Collections of the New York Historical Society. Second Series. Vol. 1, pp. 41-51.

Captain John de Verrazzano to His Most Serene Majesty the King of France, writes:[1]

Since the tempests which we encountered on the northern coasts, I have not written to your most Serene and Christian Majesty concerning the four ships sent out by your orders on the ocean to discover new lands, because I thought you must have been before apprized of all that had happened to us — that we had been compelled by the impetuous violence of the winds to put into Brittany in distress with only the two ships Normandy and Dolphin;[2] and that after having repaired these ships, we made a cruise in them, well armed, along the coast of Spain, as your Majesty must have heard, and also of our new plan of continuing our begun voyage with the Dolphin alone; from this voyage being now returned, I proceed to give your Majesty an account of our discoveries.

---

[1] This introduction reads in the original: " Captain John da Verrazzano *Florentine, of Normandy,* to the most Serene Crown of France, relates: "

[2] The signification of Delfina, the name of the Verrazzano ship of discovery, is differently given by the translators. Hakluyt renders it into English by the word Dolphin, and Dr. Cogswell here does the same. But this is not correct. The Italian for dolphin is *delfino;* which also signifies the dauphin, or oldest son of the king of France, so called because upon the cession of Dauphiny to the crown of France, he became entitled to wear the armorial device, which was a dolphin, of the princes of that province. Delfina is the feminine noun of Delfino, in that sense, that is, the Dauphiness. M. Margry has so interpreted it in this case, and accordingly gives the vessel the name of Dauphine (*Nav. Fran.*, 209), which, as she is represented to have belonged to France, would have been her actual name.

APPENDIX. 171

On the 17th of last January we set sail from a desolate rock near the island of Madeira, belonging to his most Serene Majesty the King of Portugal, with fifty men, having provisions sufficient for eight months, arms and other warlike munition and naval stores. Sailing westward with a light and pleasant easterly breeze, in twenty-five days we ran eight hundred leagues. On the 24th of February we encountered as violent a hurricane as any ship ever weathered, from which we escaped unhurt by the divine assistance and goodness, to the praise of the glorious and fortunate name of our good ship, that had been able to support the violent tossing of the waves. Pursuing our voyage towards the west, a little northwardly, in twenty-four days more, having run four hundred leagues, we reached a new country, which had never before been seen by any one, either in ancient or modern times. At first it appeared to be very low, but on approaching it to within a quarter of a league from the shore we perceived, by the great fires near the coast, that it was inhabited. We perceived that it stretched to the south, and coasted along in that direction in search of some port, in which we might come to anchor, and examine into the nature of the country, but for fifty leagues we could find none in which we could lie securely. Seeing the coast still stretched to the south, we resolved to change our course and stand to the northward, and as we still had the same difficulty, we drew in with the land and sent a boat on shore. Many people who were seen coming to the sea-side fled at our approach, but occasionally stopping, they looked back upon us with astonishment, and some were at length induced, by various friendly signs, to come to us. These showed the greatest delight on beholding us, wondering at our dress, countenances and complexion. They then showed us by signs where we could more conveniently secure our boat, and offered us some of their provisions. That your Majesty may know all that we learned, while on shore, of their manners and customs of life, I will relate what we saw as briefly as possible. They go entirely naked, except that about the loins they wear skins of small animals, like martens fastened by a girdle of plaited grass, to which they tie, all round the body, the tails of other animals hanging down to the knees; all other parts of the body and the head are naked. Some wear garlands similar to birds' feathers.

The complexion of these people is black, not much different from that of the Ethiopians; their hair is black and thick, and not very long, it is worn tied back upon the head in the form of a little tail. In person they are of good proportions, of middle stature, a little above our own, broad across the breast, strong in the arms, and well formed in the legs and other parts of the body; the only exception to their good looks is that they have broad faces, but not all, however, as we saw many that had sharp ones, with large black eyes and a fixed expression. They are not very strong in body, but acute in mind, active and swift of foot, as far as we could judge by observation. In these last two particulars they resemble the people of the east, especially those the most remote. We could not learn a great many particulars of their usages on account of our short stay among them and the distance of our ship from the shore.

We found not far from this people another whose mode of life we judged to be similar. The whole shore is covered with fine sand, about fifteen feet thick, rising in the form of little hills about fifty paces broad. Ascending farther, we found several arms of the sea which make in through inlets, washing the shores on both sides as the coast runs. An outstretched country appears at a little distance rising somewhat above the sandy shore in beautiful fields and broad plains, covered with immense forests of trees, more or less dense, too various in colours, and too delightful and charming in appearance to be described. I do not believe that they are like the Hercynian forest or the rough wilds of Scythia, and the northern regions full of vines and common trees, but adorned with palms, laurels, cypresses, and other varieties unknown in Europe, that send forth the sweetest fragrance to a great distance, but which we could not examine more closely for the reasons before given, and not on account of any difficulty in traversing the woods, which, on the contrary, are easily penetrated.

As the "East" stretches around this country, I think it cannot be devoid of the same medicinal and aromatic drugs, and various riches of gold and the like, as is denoted by the colour of the ground. It abounds also in animals, as deer, stags, hares, and many other similar, and with a great variety of birds for every kind of pleasant and delightful sports. It is plentifully supplied with lakes and ponds of running water, and being in the latitude of 34. the air is salubrious, pure and temperate, and free from the extremes of both heat and cold. There are no violent winds in these regions, the most prevalent are the north-west and west. In summer, the season in which we were there, the sky is clear, with but little rain : if fogs and mists are at any time driven in by the south wind, they are instantaneously dissipated, and at once it becomes serene and bright again. The sea is calm, not boisterous, and its waves are gentle. Although the whole coast is low and without harbours, it is not dangerous for navigation, being free from rocks and bold, so that within four or five fathoms from the shore there is twenty-four feet of water at all times of tide, and this depth constantly increases in a uniform proportion. The holding ground is so good that no ship can part her cable, however violent the wind, as we proved by experience; for while riding at anchor on the coast, we were overtaken by a gale in the beginning of March, when the winds are high, as is usual in all countries, we found our anchor broken before it started from its hold or moved at all.

We set sail from this place, continuing to coast along the shore, which we found stretching out to the west (east?); the inhabitants being numerous, we saw everywhere a multitude of fires. While at anchor on this coast, there being no harbour to enter, we sent the boat on shore with twenty-five men to obtain water, but it was not possible to land without endangering the boat, on account of the immense high surf thrown up by the sea, as it was an open roadstead. Many of the natives came to the beach, indicating by various friendly signs that we might trust ourselves on shore. One of their noble deeds of friendship deserves to be made known to your Majesty. A young sailor was attempting to swim ashore through the surf to carry them some knick-knacks, as little bells, looking-glasses, and other like trifles; when he came near three or four of them he tossed the things to them, and turned about to get back to the boat, but he was thrown over by the waves, and so dashed by them that he lay as it were dead upon the beach. When these people saw him in this situation, they ran and took him up by the head, legs and arms, and carried him to a distance from the surf; the young man, finding himself borne off in this way uttered very loud shrieks in fear and dismay, while they answered as they could in their language, showing him that he had no cause for fear. Afterwards they laid him down at the foot of a little hill, when they took off his shirt and trowsers, and examined him, expressing the greatest astonishment at the whiteness of his skin. Our sailors in the boat seeing a great fire made up, and their companion placed very near it, full of fear, as is usual in all cases of novelty, imagined that the natives were about to roast him for food. But as soon as he had recovered his strength after a short stay with them, showing by signs that he wished to return aboard, they hugged him with great affection, and accompanied him to the shore, then leaving him, that he might feel more secure, they withdrew to a little hill, from which they watched him until he was safe in the boat. This young man remarked that these people were black like the others, that they had shining skins, middle stature, and sharper faces, and very delicate bodies and limbs, and that they were inferior in strength, but quick in their minds; this is all that he observed of them.

Departing hence, and always following the shore, which stretched to the north, we came, in the space of fifty leagues, to another land, which appeared very beautiful and full of the largest forests. We approached it, and going ashore with twenty men, we went back from the coast about two leagues, and found that the people had fled and hid themselves in the woods for fear. By searching around we discovered in the grass a very old woman and a young girl of about eighteen or twenty, who had concealed themselves for the same reason; the old woman carried two infants on her shoulders, and behind her neck a little boy eight years of age; when we came up to them they began to shriek and make signs to the men who had fled to the woods. We gave them a part of our provisions, which they accepted with delight, but the girl would not touch any; every thing we offered to her being thrown down in great anger. We took the little boy from the old woman to carry with us to France, and would have taken the girl also, who was very beautiful and very tall, but it was impossible because of the loud shrieks she uttered as we attempted to lead her away; having to pass some woods, and being far from the ship, we determined to leave her and take the boy only. We found them fairer than the others, and wearing a covering made of certain plants, which hung down from the branches of the trees, tying them together with threads of wild hemp; their heads are without covering and of the same shape as the others. Their food is a kind of pulse which there abounds, different in colour and size from ours, and of a very delicious flavour. Besides they take birds and fish for food, using snares and bows made of hard wood, with reeds for arrows, in the ends of which they put the bones of fish and other animals. The animals in these regions are wilder than in Europe from being continually molested by the hunters. We saw many of their boats made of one tree twenty feet long and four feet broad, without the aid of stone or iron or other kind of metal. In the whole country, for the space of two hundred leagues, which we visited, we saw no stone of any sort. To hollow out their boats they burn out as much of a log as is requisite, and also from the prow and stern to make them float well on the sea. The land, in situation, fertility and beauty, is like the other, abounding also in forests filled with various kinds of trees, but not of such fragrance, as it is more northern and colder.

We saw in this country many vines growing naturally, which entwine about the trees, and run up upon them as they do in the plains of Lombardy. These vines would doubtless produce excellent wine if they were properly cultivated and attended to, as we have often seen the grapes which they produce very sweet and pleasant, and not unlike our own. They must be held in estimation by them, as they carefully remove the shrubbery from around them, wherever they grow, to allow the fruit to ripen better. We found also wild roses, violets, lilies, and many sorts of plants and fragrant flowers different from our own. We cannot describe their habitations, as they are in the interior of the country, but from various indications we conclude they must be formed of trees and shrubs. We saw also many grounds for conjecturing that they often sleep in the open air, without any covering but the sky. Of their other usages we know nothing; we believe, however, that all the people we were among live in the same way.

After having remained here three days, riding at anchor on the coast, as we could find no harbour, we determined to depart, and coast along the shore to the north-east, keeping sail on the vessel only by day, and coming to anchor by night. After proceeding one hundred leagues, we found a very pleasant situation among some steep hills, through which a very large river, deep at its mouth, forced its way to the sea; from the sea to the estuary of the river, any ship heavily laden might pass, with the help of the tide, which rises eight feet. But as we were riding at anchor in a good berth, we would not venture up in our vessel, without a knowledge of the mouth; therefore we took the boat, and entering the river, we found the country on its banks well peopled, the inhabitants not differing much from the others, being dressed out with feathers of birds of various colours. They came towards us with evident delight, raising loud shouts of admiration, and showing us where we could most securely land with our boat. We passed up this river, about half a league, when we found it formed a most beautiful lake three leagues in circuit, upon which they were rowing thirty or more of their small boats, from one shore to the other, filled with multitudes who came to see us. All of a sudden, as is wont to happen to navigators, a violent contrary wind blew in from the sea, and forced us to return to our ship, greatly regretting to leave this region which seemed so commodious and delightful, and which we supposed must also contain great riches, as the hills showed many indications of minerals. Weighing anchor, we sailed *eighty* (ottanta) leagues towards the east, as the coast stretched in that direction, and always in sight of it; at length we discovered an island of a triangular form, about ten leagues from the mainland, in size about equal to the island of Rhodes, having many hills covered with trees, and well peopled, judging from the great number of fires which we saw all around its shores; we gave it the name of your Majesty's illustrious mother.

We did not land there, as the weather was unfavourable, but proceeded to another place, fifteen leagues distant from the island, where we found a very excellent harbour. Before entering it, we saw about twenty small boats full of people, who came about our ship, uttering many cries of astonishment, but they would not approach nearer than within fifty paces; stopping, they looked at the structure of our ship, our persons and dress, afterwards they all raised a loud shout together, signifying that they were pleased. By imitating their signs, we inspired them in some measure with confidence, so that they came near enough for us to toss to them some little bells and glasses, and many toys, which they took and looked at, laughing, and then came on board without fear. Among them were two kings more beautiful in form and stature than can possibly be described; one was about forty years old, the other about twenty-four, and they were dressed in the following manner: The oldest had a deer's skin around his body, artificially wrought in damask figures, his head was without covering, his hair was tied back in various knots; around his neck he wore a large chain ornamented with many stones of different colours. The young man was similar in his general appearance. This is the finest looking tribe, and the handsomest in their costumes, that we have found in our voyage. They exceed us in size, and they are of a very fair complexion (?); some of them incline more to a white (bronze?), and others to a tawny colour; their faces are sharp, their hair long and black, upon the adorning of which they bestow great pains; their eyes are black and sharp, their expression mild and pleasant, greatly resembling the antique. I say nothing to your Majesty of the other parts of the body, which are all in good proportion, and such as belong to well-formed men. Their women are of the same form and beauty, very graceful, of fine countenances and pleasing appearance in manners and modesty; they wear no clothing except a deer skin, ornamented like those worn by the men; some wear very rich lynx skins upon their arms, and various ornaments upon their heads, composed of braids of hair, which also hang down upon their breasts on each side. Others wear different ornaments, such as the women of Egypt and Syria use. The older and the married people, both men and women, wear many ornaments in their ears, hanging down in the oriental manner. We saw upon them several pieces of wrought copper, which is more esteemed by them than gold, as this is not valued on account of its colour, but is considered by them as the most ordinary of the metals—yellow being the colour especially disliked by them; azure and red are those in highest estimation with them. Of those things which we gave them, they prized most highly the bells, azure crystals, and other toys to hang in their ears and about their necks; they do not value or care to have silk or gold stuffs, or other kinds of cloth, nor implements of steel or iron. When we showed them our arms, they expressed no admiration, and only asked how they were made; the same was the case with the looking-glasses, which they returned to us, smiling, as soon as they had looked at them. They are very generous, giving away whatever they have. We formed a great friendship with them, and one day we entered into the port with our ship, having before rode at the distance of a league from the shore, as the weather was adverse. They came off to the ship with a number of their little boats, with their faces painted in divers colours, showing us real signs of joy, bringing us of their provisions, and signifying to us where we could best ride in safety with our ship; and keeping with us until we had cast anchor. We remained among them fifteen days, to provide ourselves with many things of which we were in want, during which time they came every day to see our ship, bringing with them their wives, of whom they were very careful; for, although they came on board themselves, and remained a long while, they made their wives stay in the boats, nor could we ever get them on board by any entreaties or any presents we could make them. One of the two kings often came with his queen and many attendants, to see us for his amusement; but he always stopped at the distance of about two hundred paces and sent a boat to inform us of his intended visit, saying they would come and see our ship — this was done for safety, and as soon as they had an answer from us they came off, and remained awhile to look around; but on hearing the annoying cries of the sailors, the king sent the queen, with her attendants, in a very light boat, to wait, near an island a quarter of a league distant from us, while he remained a long time on board, talking with us by signs, and expressing his fanciful notions about every thing in the ship, and asking the use of all. After imitating our modes of salutation, and tasting our food, he courteously took leave of us. Sometimes, when our men staid two or three days on a small island, near the ship, for their various necessities, as sailors are wont to do, he came with seven or eight of his attendants, to enquire about our movements, often asking us if we intended to remain there long, and offering us every thing at his command, and then he would shoot with his bow, and run up and down with his people, making great sport for us. We often went five or six leagues into the interior, and found the country as pleasant as is possible to conceive, adapted to cultivation of every kind, whether of corn, wine or oil; there are open plains twenty-five or thirty leagues in extent, entirely free from trees or other hinderances, and of so great fertility, that whatever is sown there will yield an excellent crop. On entering the woods, we observed that they might all be traversed by an army ever so numerous; the trees of which they were composed, were oaks, cypresses, and others, unknown in Europe. We found, also, apples, plumbs, filberts, and many other fruits, but all of a different kind from ours. The animals, which are in great numbers, as stags, deer, lynxes, and many other species, are taken by snares, and by bows, the latter being their chief implement; their arrows are wrought with great beauty, and for the heads of them, they use emery, jasper, hard marble, and other sharp stones, in the place of iron. They also use the same kind of sharp stones in cutting down trees, and with them they construct their boats of single logs, hollowed out with admirable skill, and sufficiently commodious to contain ten or twelve persons; their oars are short, and broad at the end, and are managed in rowing by force of the arms alone, with perfect security, and as nimbly as they choose. We saw their dwellings, which are of a circular form, of about ten or twelve paces in circumference, made of logs split in halves, without any regularity of architecture, and covered with roofs of straw, nicely put on, which protect them from wind and rain. There is no doubt that they would build stately edifices if they had workmen as skilful as ours, for the whole sea-coast abounds in shining stones, crystals, and alabaster, and for the same reason it has ports and retreats for animals. They change their habitations from place to place as circumstances of situation and season may require; this is easily done, as they have only to take with them their mats, and they have other houses prepared at once. The father and the whole family dwell together in one house in great numbers; in some we saw twenty-five or thirty persons. Their food is pulse, as with the other tribes, which is here better than elsewhere, and more carefully cultivated; in the time of sowing they are governed by the moon, the sprouting of grain, and many other ancient usages. They live by hunting and fishing, and they are long-lived. If they fall sick, they cure themselves without medicine, by the heat of the fire, and their death at last comes from extreme old age. We judge them to be very affectionate and charitable towards their relatives—making loud lamentations in their adversity, and in their misery calling to mind all their good fortune. At their departure out of life, their relations mutually join in weeping, mingled with singing, for a long while. This is all that we could learn of them. This region is situated in the parallel of Rome, being 41° 40′ of north latitude, but much colder from accidental circumstances, and not by nature, as I shall hereafter explain to your Majesty, and confine myself at present to the description of its local situation. It looks towards the south, on which side the

APPENDIX. 181

harbour is half a league broad; afterwards upon entering it, the extent between the *cast* (oriente) and north is twelve leagues,[1] and then enlarging itself it forms a very large bay, twenty leagues in circumference, in which are five small islands, of great fertility and beauty, covered with large and lofty trees. Among these islands any fleet, however large, might ride safely, without fear of tempests or other dangers. Turning towards the south, at the entrance of the harbour, on both sides, there are very pleasant hills, and many streams of clear water, which flow down to the sea. In the midst of the entrance there is a rock of freestone, formed by nature, and suitable for the construction of any kind of machine or bulwark for the defence of the harbour.

Having supplied ourselves with every thing necessary, on the *sixth* (sei) of May we departed from the port, and sailed one hundred and fifty leagues, keeping so close to the coast as never to lose it from our sight; the nature of the country appeared much the same as before, but the mountains were a little higher, and all in appearance rich in minerals. We did not stop to land as the weather was very favourable for pursuing our voyage, and the country presented no variety. The shore stretched to the east, and fifty leagues beyond more to the north, where we found a more elevated country, full of very thick woods of fir trees, cypresses and the like, indicative of a cold climate. The people were entirely different from the others we had seen, whom we had found kind and gentle, but these were so rude and barbarous that we were unable by any signs we could make, to hold communication with them. They clothe themselves in the skins of bears, lynxes, seals and other animals. Their food, as far as we could judge by several visits to their dwellings, is obtained by hunting and fishing, and fruits, which are a sort of root of spontaneous growth. They have no pulse, and we saw no signs of cultivation; the land appears sterile and unfit for growing of fruit or grain of any kind. If we wished at any time to traffick with them, they came to the sea shore and stood upon the rocks, from which they

---

[1] See *ante*, p. 51, *note*.

lowered down by a cord to our boats beneath whatever they had to barter, continually crying out to us, not to come nearer, and instantly demanding from us that which was to be given in exchange; they took from us only knives, fish hooks and sharpened steel. No regard was paid to our courtesies; when we had nothing left to exchange with them, the men at our departure made the most brutal signs of disdain and contempt possible. Against their will we penetrated two or three leagues into the interior with twenty-five men; when we came to the shore, they shot at us with their arrows, raising the most horrible cries and afterwards fleeing to the woods. In this region we found nothing extraordinary except vast forests and some metalliferous hills, as we infer from seeing that many of the people wore copper ear-rings. Departing from thence, we kept along the coast, steering north-east, and found the country more pleasant and open, free from woods, and distant in the interior we saw lofty mountains, but none which extended to the shore. Within fifty leagues we discovered thirty-two islands, all near the main land, small and of pleasant appearance, but high and so disposed as to afford excellent harbours and channels, as we see in the Adriatic gulph, near Illyria and Dalmatia. We had no intercourse with the people, but we judge that they were similar in nature and usages to those we were last among. After sailing between east and north the distance of one hundred and fifty leagues more, and finding our provisions and naval stores nearly exhausted, we took in wood and water and determined to return to France, having discovered 502,[1] that is 700 (sic) leagues of unknown lands.

As to the religious faith of all these tribes, not understanding their language, we could not discover either by sign or gestures any thing certain. It seemed to us that they had no religion or laws, or any knowledge of a First Cause or Mover, that they worshipped neither the heavens, stars, sun, moon nor other planets; nor could we learn if they were given to any kind of idolatry, or offered any sacrifices or supplications, or if they have

---

[1] See *ante*, p. 58, *note*.

temples or houses of prayer in their villages;—our conclusion was, that they have no religious belief whatever, but live in this respect entirely free. All which proceeds from ignorance, as they are very easy to be persuaded, and imitated us with earnestness and fervour in all which they saw us do as Christians in our acts of worship.

It remains for me to lay before your Majesty a Cosmographical exposition of our voyage. Taking our departure, as I before observed, from the above mentioned desert rocks, which lie on the extreme verge of the west, as known to the ancients, in the meridian of the Fortunate Islands, and in the latitude of 32 degrees north from the equator, and steering a westward course, we had run, when we first made land, a distance of 1200 leagues or 4800 miles, reckoning, according to nautical usage, four miles to a league. This distance calculated geometrically, upon the usual ratio of the diameter to the circumference of the circle, gives 92 degrees; for if we take 114 degrees as the chord of an arc of a great circle, we have by the same ratio 95 deg., as the chord of an arc on the parallel of 34 degrees, being that on which we first made land, and 300 degrees as the circumference of the whole circle passing through this plane. Allowing then, as actual observations show, that $62\frac{1}{2}$ terrestrial miles correspond to a celestial degree, we find the whole circumference of 300 deg., as just given, to be 18,759 miles, which divided by 360, makes the length of a degree of longitude in the parallel of 34 degrees to be 52 miles, and that is the true measure. Upon this basis, 1200 leagues, or 4800 miles meridional distance, on the parallel of 34, give 92 degrees, and so many therefore have we sailed farther to the west than was known to the ancients. During our voyage we had no lunar eclipses or like celestial phenomenas, we therefore determined our progress from the difference of longitude, which we ascertained by various instruments, by taking the sun's altitude from day to day, and by calculating geometrically the distance run by the ship from one horizon to another; all these observations, as also the ebb and flow of the sea in all places, were noted in a little book, which may prove serviceable to navigators; they are communicated to your Majesty in the hope of promoting science.

My intention in this voyage was to reach Cathay, on the extreme coast of Asia, expecting however, to find in the newly discovered land some such an obstacle, as they have proved to be, yet I did not doubt that I should penetrate by some passage to the eastern ocean. It was the opinion of the ancients, that our oriental Indian ocean is one and without interposing land; Aristotle supports it by arguments founded on various probabilities; but it is contrary to that of the moderns and shown to be erroneous by experience; the country which has been discovered, and which was unknown to the ancients, is another world compared with that before known, being manifestly larger than our Europe, together with Africa and perhaps Asia, if we might rightly estimate its extent, as shall now be briefly explained to your Majesty. The Spaniards have sailed south beyond the equator on a meridian 20 degrees west of the Fortunate Islands to the latitude of 54, and there still found land; turning about they steered northward on the same meridian and along the coast to the eighth degree of latitude near the equator, and thence along the coast more to the west and north-west, to the latitude of 21°, without finding a termination to the continent; they estimated the distance run as 89 degrees, which, added to the 20 first run west of the Canaries, make 109 degrees and so far west; they sailed from the meridian of these islands, but this may vary somewhat from truth; we did not make this voyage and therefore cannot speak from experience; we calculated it geometrically from the observations furnished by many navigators, who have made the voyage and affirm the distance to be 1600 leagues, due allowance being made for the deviations of the ship from a straight course, by reason of contrary winds. I hope that we shall now obtain certain information on these points, by new voyages to be made on the same coasts. But to return to ourselves; in the voyage which we have made by order of your Majesty, in addition to the 92 degrees we run towards the west from our point of departure, before we reached land in the latitude of 34, we have to count 300 leagues which we ran north-east-wardly, and 400 nearly east along the coast before we reached the 50th parallel of north latitude, the point where we turned our course from the shore towards home. Beyond this point the Portuguese had already sailed as far north as the Arctic circle, without coming to the termination of the land. Thus adding the degrees of south latitude explored, which are 54, to those of the north, which are 66, the sum is 120, and therefore, more than are embraced in the latitude of Africa and Europe, for the north point of Norway, which is the extremity of Europe, is in 71 north, and the Cape of Good Hope, which is the southern extremity of Africa, is in 35 south, and their sum is only 106, and if the breadth of this newly discovered country corresponds to its extent of sea coast, it doubtless exceeds Asia in size. In this way we find that the land forms a much larger portion of our globe than the ancients supposed, who maintained, contrary to mathematical reasoning, that it was less than the water, whereas actual experience proves the reverse, so that we judge in respect to extent of surface the land covers as much space as the water; and I hope more clearly and more satisfactorily to point out and explain to your Majesty the great extent of that new land, or new world, of which I have been speaking. The continent of Asia and Africa, we know for certain is joined to Europe at the north in Norway and Russia, which disproves the idea of the ancients that all this part had been navigated from the Cimbric Chersonesus, eastward as far as the Caspian Sea. They also maintained that the whole continent was surrounded by two seas situate to the east and west of it, which seas in fact do not surround either of the two continents, for as we have seen above, the land of the southern hemisphere at the latitude of 54 extends eastwardly an unknown distance, and that of the northern passing the 66th parallel turns to the east, and has no termination as high as the 70th. In a short time, I hope, we shall have more certain knowledge of these things, by the aid of your Majesty, whom I pray Almighty God to prosper in lasting glory, that we may see the most important results of this our cosmography in the fulfilment of the holy words of the Gospel.

On board the ship Dolphin, in the port of Dieppe in Normandy, the 8th of July, 1524.

Your humble servitor,
JANUS VERRAZZANUS.

ERRATA.

On pages 49, 72, 79, and 116 for Dauphiny read *Dauphine*.

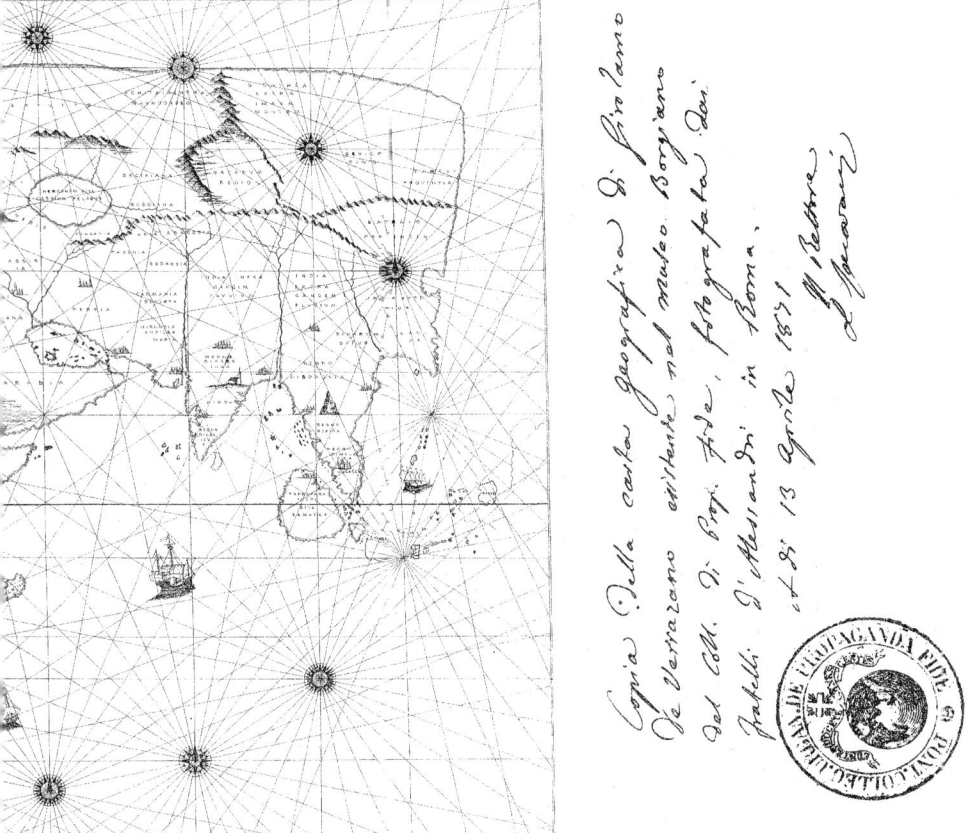

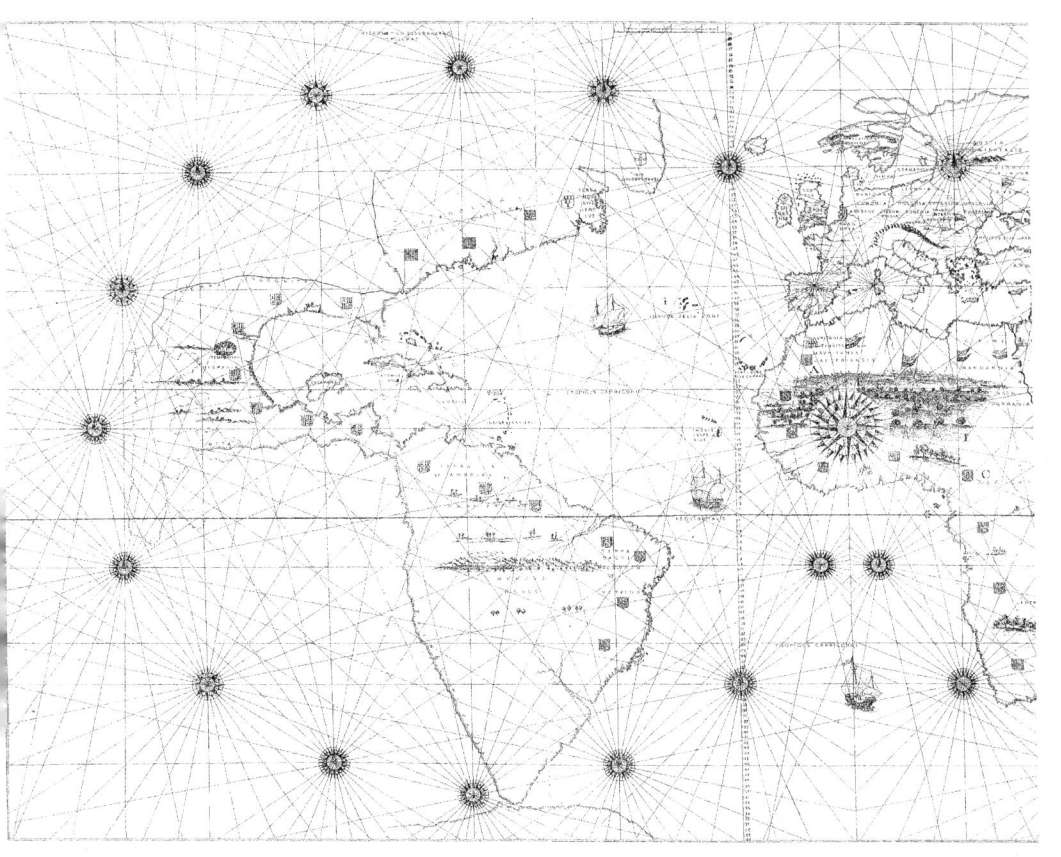

From Photographs of the Original, preserved in the MUSEO BORGIANO at the Collegio Rom

INDEX.

A.

Acadia, granted to the Sieur de Monts, 40.
Adventurers with Verrazzano at the time of his capture, 148, 167.
Agnese, Baptista, his map showing the western sea, 88, 100, 105.
Ailly, Pierre d', table of climates, 63.
Albemarle, North Carolina, coast of, 48.
Alfonse, Jean, chief pilot of Roberval, his cosmography, 37; description and chart of Norumbega, 38 ; explores the coast of New England, 39 ; his book of voyages, 39.
Algonkin Indians, their birch-bark canoe, 75, 83 ; not cannibals, 149.
Alonzo, Domingo, sent to the Azores for the treasure, 143.
Andrade, extract from his Chronicle of João III, in relation to Verrazzano, 139, 145.
Ango, Jean, father and son, rich and powerful merchants of Dieppe, connected with Verrazzano, 35, 86, 144, 146, 158, 160.
Anonymous Portuguese chart, followed by the Verrazano map, 97, 98.
Anonymous Spanish chart, of 1527 showing the exploration of Gomez, 123.
Arcangeli, M., discourse on Verrazzano, 13, 17, 108.
Arctic Circle, Portuguese discoveries towards the, 58, 66, 67.
Arecifes, on Ribero's map, Cape Sable in Nova Scotia, 131.
Aubert, Thomas, of Dieppe, voyage to Newfoundland in 1508, carries Indians thence to France, 62-3, 75, 87.
Avorobagra, on the French map, supposed to be the same as Norumbega, 43.
Ayllon, first expedition in 1521 to the river Jordan or Santee carries sixty Indians thence to St. Domingo, 78, 123 ; he takes one to Spain, 124 ; second expedition in 1526 explores no further north than the Jordan, 123-4 ; dies at St. Helena, 123.

B.

Bacalao, Bacalaos, Baccalaos Bacallaos and Baccallaos, or Newfoundland 61, 94, 122, 131.
Badajos, Gomez a member of the junta, 120.
Barcia, description of the exploration of Menendez Marquez to the Chesapeake, 50; identifies Verrazzano with Juan Florin, 136, 148.
Basle, Sebastian Münster's edition of Ptolemy, printed at, 101, 103-4.
Beaufort, N. C., an accessible harbor, 48.

188 VERRAZZANO.

Belleforest, François de, the first historian in France who mentions in print the Verrazzano voyage, 28, 29.
Belle Isle, route of Cartier through the straits, 29, 62.
Bergeron, takes his account of the Verrazzano voyage from Lescarbot, 29.
Block island, not intended by the island of Louise, 53.
Bodleian library, portolano based on the Ribero map, 106.
Borgia, Cardinal Stefano, possessor of the Verrazano map, 91.
Bourbon, Charles de, the constable, invades France with Pescara, 21, 22.
Boy, the Indian, mentioned in the Verrazzano letter, 5, 20.
Brazil, threatened voyage to, by Verrazzano, 139 ; voyage abandoned, 145.
Bretons, early discoveries in North America, 62, 65–8, 86.
Brevoort, J. C., notes on the Verrazano map, 4, 95, 102.
Bristol, bark canoe taken to, in 1603, 75.
Brittany, arms of, 94 ; fishermen of, 100.

C.

Cabot, Sebastian, 72, 113, 117 ; his opinion of the insular character of Northern America, 119, 120, 134.
Cabral, publication in France of his discoveries, 33.
California, black Indians found in, 78.
Canada, discovered by Jacques Cartier, 32, 34–6 ; grant of, to Marquis de la Roche, 37 ; first permanent settlements in, by Sieur de Monts, 40–1.
Canoes, birch-bark, peculiar to the northern Indians, 75, 83, 90.
Cape Breton, 38, 57–8, 60–3 ; why so called, 86 ; 97–8, 104, 131.
Cape Cod, 52, 54, 56, 75 ; C. de Muchas Yllas on the Ribero map, 130–2.
Cape de Ras, 86, 90 ; Cabo Raso, 61, 94, 131 ; Cape Race, 57, 59, 62, 131.
Cape Roman, S. C., southerly limit of the Verrazzano voyage, 1 ; Cape de S. Roman on the Ribero map, 130.
Cape Fear, the Verrazzano landfall near, 47 ; C. Traffalgar on the Ribero map, 130.
Cape Hatteras, 48 ; C. de S. Juan on the Ribero map, 130.
Cape Sable, Nova Scotia, Cap de Noroveregue on the chart of Alfonse, 38, 56 ; Arecifes on the map of Ribero, 131–2.
Cape St. Vincent, treasure captured by Verrazzano near, 143.
Caravel, depicted, 9 ; described, 47–8.
Carli, Fernando, alleged letter to his father, 11, 16, 17, 155 ; his version of the Verrazzano letter, 11, 12, 65, 170.
Caro, Annibal, letter mentioning a Verrazzano map, 91, 108, 115.
Cartier Jacques, voyages through the straits of Belle-Isle, 29, 39 ; silent as to Verrazzano, 30 ; his voyages, 32, 34, 44, 46, 59, 103, 105 ; inland sea mentioned by him, 107.
Castles, gulf of the, or straits of Belle-Isle, 86, 90.
Cathay, 17, 97, 119 ; proposed voyage of Verrazzano, 141, 145.
Catholic navigators, custom in regard to naming places, 46.
Cespedes, history of islands of the world, 121, 133.
Chabot, Phillipe, Sieur de Brion, Admiral of France, enters into a venture with Verrazzano, 35, 137, 146, 158, 160 ; superseded by the dauphin, afterwards Henry II, 42.

INDEX. 189

Charlevoix, cites Ramusio alone for the voyage, 4, 30.
Chesapeake bay, the, 40, 48, 49; called the bay of Santa Maria, and explored by Menendez Marquez in 1573, 50; entrance into, 56, 121, 135.
Claudia, island of, so first named by Mercator, 107, 110.
Clement VII, pope, map of Ribero presented to him in 1529, 124.
Cogswell, Dr. J. G., translation of the Carli version of the Verrazzano letter, 13, 51, 127, 170.
Colines, Simon de, printer in Paris in 1525, 33.
Colmenar de Arenas, near Puerto del Pico, Verrazzano executed at, 148, 167.
Columbus, Christopher, 31-2, 48, 70.
Columbus, Bartholomew, 71.
Complexion of the Indians misstated in the Verrazzano letter, 76.
Contarini, Venetian Ambassador, letter in relation to Sebastian Cabot, 113.
Coronelli, on the place of death of Verrazzano, 135.
Corsair the profession of Verrazzano, 137.
Cortereal, Gaspar, voyage of, 22, 59, 60, 95.
Cortereaes, voyage of the brothers, 61.
Cortes, treasure sent by him from Mexico to the emperor, captured by Verrazzano, 142-3.
Corunna, Gomez sails on his voyage of discovery from, 120.
Cosmography of the Verrazzano letter, 7, 16; of Jean Alfonse, 37.

D.

Dauphin, afterwards Henry II, admiral of France, 42; arms of, 42, 44.
Dauphine, the Verrazzano vessel of discovery, 3, 47, 49, 72, 79, 116, 170.
D'Avezac, M., on the early French map, 41; the Dieppe Captain, 85, 125.
Davila, Alonzo, custodian of the treasure sent by Cortes captured by Verrazzano, 142; his letter giving an account of the capture, 143, 164.
Delaware bay, explored by Gomez, 121.
Denys, Jean, voyage in 1504 from Honfleur to Newfoundland, 86.
Desertas, rocks near Madeira, whence the Verrazzano voyage of discovery began, 3, 7, 58.
Diaz, Bernal, on the capture of Verrazzano, 147-8.
Dieppa laid down on the Verrazano map, 93, 95, 135-6.
Dieppe in Normandy, Verrazzano a denizen of, 3, 64, 136, 143-4.
Dieppe, discourse of the French captain of, 37, 62, 67, 84.

E.

Elizabeth islands, near Cape Cod, 52; natives of, 78-9; termination of the fourth course of the Verrazzano voyage, 130.
Esquimaux, voyage of Cortereal among the, 60.
Estienne Henri, early printer in Paris, 31, 33, 62.
Ethiopians, Indians represented in the Verrazzano letter to have been black like them, 76.
Eusebius' Chronicle by Multivallis, account of the Indians taken in 1508 from Newfoundland to France, 62-3.

F.

Fabre's translation of Pigafetta's journal, by order of Louise, 15, 33.
Florida, discovered by the Spaniards, 93.
Florin, Juan, a French corsair, identified as Verrazzano, 136–7; captures a ship from Hispaniola, 138; also the treasure sent by Cortes, 143, 145; takes a Portuguese ship coming from the Indies, 145; list of his vessels, 165.
France, no evidence of the Verrazzano voyage ever found there, 26.
Francese, Francisca or the French land, 88, 103, 105.
Francis I, king of France, Verrazzano letter addressed to, 3, 170; his movements at the time it purports to bear date, 21; absent from his capital or a prisoner in Spain from June 1524 until early in 1526, 22, 23; never recognized the Verrazzano discovery, 34; and lived for 23 years after it is alleged to have taken place, without asserting any right under it; but otherwise attempting colonization in America, 35, 41.
Francis, the Chicorane, his false stories about the country to Ayllon, 124.
French captain of Dieppe, discourse of, 57, 62, 67, 84; who he was, 85.
French cartographer of the reign of Francis excludes the Verrazzano discovery, 41–4.
French fishermen frequented Newfoundland and Cape Breton, before the Verrazzano voyage, 63.
French navigation to the northern coast of America, 100, 106.
Fundy, bay of, 54, 56.

G.

Gamos, Rio de, the Penobscot, explored by Gomez, 121, 133.
Garcia, Nuño, Spanish cartographer, his map, 126.
Gastaldi, his map representing Norumbega, 38; and Acadia, 40; author of the maps in Ramusio, 92.
Georgetown, S. C., harbor, 48.
Giles, Juan de, judge at Cadiz, executes the death warrant upon Verrazzano, 148; his letters to the emperor, 167–8.
Globe of Ulpius containing the Verrazzano legend, 99, 101, 103, 113.
Gomez, Estévan, Portuguese pilot, enters the Spanish service, 117; accompanies Magellan as chief pilot and deserts him, 118; attends the junta at Badajos, 120; sails in 1525 on a voyage of discovery to North America for the emperor, 120; explores the coast from Cape Roman to Cape Breton, 120–1; his voyage described by Oviedo in the following year, and his exploration laid down in 1527 and 1529 on Spanish charts, 122–3; which were known before the Verrazzano letter is shown to have existed, 126; and were the basis of that letter, 126.
Gosnold's voyage to Cape Cod, 78.

Grapes alleged in the Verrazzano letter to have been ripe in North Carolina in April, 5, 80, 81, 82.
Greene, George W., his monograph on Verrazzano, 14; asserts the recomposition of the Verrazzano letter in Ramusio, 14, 16.
Gualdape, or St. Helena, S. C., river visited by Ayllon, where he dies, 123.

H.

Hakluyt, reprints Ribault's Terra Florida, 27; publishes map of Michael Lok, 101; his mention of Verrazzano, 109-111, 146; translation of the letter mentioned, 110, 137, 170.
Harrisse, M., publishes the commission of Roberval, 36.
Hatteras, Cape, 48; C. de S. Juan on the Ribero map, 130.
Henry VIII, of England, sends an expedition to Newfoundland in 1527, 63, 113; map presented to him by Verrazzano, 109-112.
Henry, Dauphin, 42; King Henry II, 36, 41.
Henry III, of France, 37.
Henry IV, of France, 37.
Henry, Cape, at the entrance of the Chesapeake, 49, 56.
Hispaniola, natives, 70; map, 126; ship captured by Verrazzano, 138.
Hochelaga, grant, 37; river, 38.
Homem, Diego, map acknowledges that of Ribero, 106.
Hudson river, shown on the map of Ribero, 43, 121, 130, 132.

I.

Indians of North America, complexion of, 78, 79, 82.
Indians carried to Rouen in 1508-9, 62-3; to Toledo by Gomez, 122.
Indies, proposed voyage by Verrazzano to the, 145-7.
Iucatanet, or Nova Gallia on the Verrazzano map, 95.
Italy, discoveries of Gomez immediately made known in, 124.
Itinerary of Charles V, 148-9.

J.

Jomard, M., repoduces a French map of the Verrazzano period, 41.
Jordan, the river Santee, most northerly point reached by the expeditions of Ayllon, 123-4.
João III, king of Portugal, extract in regard to Verrazzano, from the chronicle of, 139; letter of Silveira to, 162.

K.

Kohl, J. G., geographical works and observations, 88, 101, 102, 105, 123.
Kunstmann, von Spruner and Thomas, their atlas published at Munich, 62.

L.

Labrador, grant of, 37; Jean Alfonse there, 39.
Landfall of the Verrazzano voyage, 4, 5, 47, 130.
Laudoniere, uses the version of Ramusio, 27–8.
La Plata, voyage of Sebastian Cabot, 120.
Laurentian library in Florence, 15.
League, length according to the Verrazzano letter, 47, 129.
Le Clerc mistakes as to the discovery of the straits of Belle Isle by Alfonse, 39.
Leri, Baron de, fabulous visit to the island of Sable, 40.
Lerma, order of execution of Verrazzano made by Charles V at, 148.
Lescarbot, plagiarist as to the voyage of Verrazzano, 29.
Livorno, Leghorn, on the Verrazano map, 93, 95.
Long Island, 52, 55.
Lok or Locke, Michael, map of, 101–2, 109–110.
Louise of Savoy, mother of Francis I, island called after, 6; made regent, 27; causes Pigafetta's journal of Magellan's voyage to be translated, 32–3; her death, 10; referred to in the discourse of the French captain, 87.
Luisia, island of, on the Verrazzano map, 94.

M.

Madeira, the Dauphine leaves there on her voyage of discovery, 4, 79.
Madrid, treaty of in 1526, 147.
Magellan, 15, 18; journal of his voyage presented to Louise, 32–3; straits of first represented on the Ptolemaic maps by Münster, 104; his expedition from Spain, 118; death, 119.
Magliabechian library in Florence, Verrazzano letter in the, 15, 170.
Maine, bay of, 54.
Marcellus Cervinus, bishop of Florence, cardinal and pope, globe constructed for by Ulpius, 114, 150.
Mare de Verrazzana, 102, 109.
Mare Occidentale, 96, 102.
Margaux, wild fowl on the coast of Newfoundland, 90.
Margry, M. adopts the Carli version of the letter, 30; first publishes the agreement between Chabot and Verrazzano, 146, 158; his interpretation of the name of the Verrazano vessel, 170.
Martha's Vineyard, island of, 53; Indians of, 79, 130.
Martyr, Peter, decades of, translated into French and printed in Paris, 32; account of natives of the West India islands, 72; describes the complexion of the Indians of South Carolina, 78; mentions the proposed expedition of Gomez, 120; his history of the West Indies, 125; his mention of Juan Florin, 136, 138, 142, 143, 145.
Massachusetts bay, 54–5, 69.

INDEX. 193

Matienzo and Ayllon, expedition of, 78, 123.
Menendez, Pedro, the adelantado, 50.
Menendez Marquez Pedro, explores the coast from the point of Florida to the Chesapeake, 50.
Mercator, the first cartographer to refer to Verrazzano, 101, 107.
Micmacs, natives of Cape Breton, 63.
Moluccas, new route proposed by Gomez, 117.
Moncada, Hugo de, commander of the Spanish fleet in Barbary, 17, 19, 22.
Montana verde, on the map of Ribero, the highlands of Navesink at the mouth of the Hudson, 130, 132; copied on the map of Ruscelli, 106.
Montezuma, articles belonging to, 143.
Monts, Seiur de, Canada first colonized under his grants, 40.
Muchas yllas, C. de, or Cape Cod, 130-2.
Munich atlas, 61-2, (*note*), 97.
Münster, Sebastian, map in his works, 102, 103, 105.

N.

Nantucket, island of, 54, 130.
Narraganset, bay of, not referred to in the Verrazzano letter, 52, 55; Indians, 73, 79.
Nasquapees, natives of Labrador, 63.
Navarrete, error as to the voyage of Ayllon, 123.
Navesink, the highlands of, recognized, 49, 130.
Newfoundland, 37-8, 57, 61; resorted by the French and Portuguees. before the Verrazzano voyage, 61-4; red Indians of, 63, 90.
New England, coast of, explored by Jean Alfonse, 38-9; part of Acadia, 40, 55; early French navigation to, 100.
New France, first attempt to colonize, 36; map of 92.
Newport, its harbor not intended in the Verrazzano letter, 53.
Normands and Bretons, in 1504 discover Newfoundland, 62, 86; resort there to fish, 63-4.
Normanda, name of one of the Verrazzano fleet, 3.
Normandy, fishermen of, in Newfoundland, 63-4; fleet preparing in the ports of, 139-42; Verrazzano a denizen of, 170.
Noroveregue, cape of, Cape Sable, 88.
North Carolina, landfall of the Verrazzano voyage, 47; harbor of Beaufort, 48; natives, 69, 79; ripening of grapes, 81.
Norumbega, land of, 36; described by Jean Alfonse, 37-8; map of, 37-8; discovered by the Portuguese and Spaniards, 39; an Indian name, 38, 87.

O.

Ochelaga, country of, 36; river of, 88.
Olimpe, C. de, on the Verrazzano map, 93.
Oviedo, on the custom of naming newly discovered places, 46; his account of the voyage of Gomez, 82, 121-2, 125, 136.

P.

Paesi novamente ritrovati, Italian book of voyages translated and printed in Paris, 32.
Pamlico sound, complexion of the natives, 78.
Paris, early printing, 31–2.
Parmentier, Jean, voyage to Sumatra, 85, 147.
Pasqualigo, the Venetian ambassador, account of the voyage of Cortereal, 59.
Pelli, life of Verrazzano, 12, 134.
Peltry, early trade in, to Norumbega, 38.
Penobscot, called the river of Norumbega and described by Alfonse, 37–8 ; explored first by Gomez and called by him rio de los Gamos, 121, 133.
Pensee, a ship of Dieppe, voyage to Newfoundland, 86.
Pescara, army of, in Provencê in 1524, 21–2.
Pigafetta, journal of Magellan's voyage, translated by order of Louise, 15, 32–3.
Portuguese, discoveries of the, 58, 59, 86; charts of, 61, 65–7; fishermen in Newfoundland, 61–3.
Printing well established in France in the time of Verrazzano, 31–2.
Pringe, Capt. Martin, his description of the birch-bark canoe, 75 ; and of the complexion of the Indians of Martha's Vineyard, 79.
Propaganda, college of the, Verrazzano map in its possession, 17.
Provence, invasion of, by the army of the emperor, 22.
Ptolemy, edition of, by Bernardus Sylvanus, showing Newfoundland, in 1511, 60 ; by Sebastian Münster printed in 1540 at Basle, showing Canada, 101–3.
Puerto del Pico, Verrazzano executed at Colmenar, near, 148.

Q.

Quejo, Pedro de, pilot of Matienzo, testimony as to his expedition, 123.
Quiñones, Antonio, custodian of treasure sent to Spain by Cortes, 142 ; killed in the action with Verrazzano, 143.

R.

Race, Cape, 57, 59, 61–2, 94, 131.
Ramusio, first publishes the Verrazzano letter, 2, 10 ; recomposes it and materially alters the text, 4, 55, 82–3, 137; for three centuries the only authority for the voyage, 13, 30, 33, 65, 67 ; responsible for the credit given to the letter, 83 ; edits a translation in Italian of Oviedo's first work, 125 ; his account of the death of Verrazzano an imposition, 134–5, 149–50.
Raso, Cabo, 61, 94, 131.

Red Indians of Newfoundland, why so called, 63.
Regiomontanus, his table of eclipses, 8.
Reinel, Pedro, map of, 61, 97.
Rhode Island, complexion of the Indians of, 78.
Rhodes, similar island named after the mother of Francis, 6, 21, 52.
Ribault, derives his information in regard to Verrazzano, from Ramusio, 26–7.
Ribera, Juan, secretary of Cortes, carries the news to Spain of the treasure at the Azores, 142, 144.
Ribero, Diego, Spanish cartographer, map of, 43, 50, 100 ; lays down the exploration of Gomez, 121–3 ; his map in 1529 presented to the pope, 124 ; and is the basis of the Verrazzano letter, 126–133.
Rio de Buelta, on Cape Breton, northerly limit of the voyage of Gomez, 120.
Rio de los Gamos, the Penobscot, explored by Gomez, 121.
Roberval, expedition to Canada, 34–6 ; his commission first published by M. Harrisse, 36 ; his return from Canada in 1543, 41–2.
Roche, Marquis de la, commissions to settle the newly discovered countries, 36–7 ; his failure, 39, 40.
Rochelle, Verrazzano at, 143–4 ; letter of Alonzo Davila from, 164–5.
Rosier, account of the New England Indians using tobacco, 74.
Rouen, Indians of Newfoundland, with their birch-bark canoe, taken there in 1608, 62.
Ruscelli, map of, refers to the discoveries of Gomez, 106.
Rut, John, voyage to Newfoundland in 1527, 63, 113.

S.

Sable, Cape, Nova Scotia, called Cape of Norumbega, by Alfonse, 38, 56 ; Arecifes on Ribero's map, 131–2.
Sable island, convicts abandoned there by de la Roche, 40.
Saggiatore, a journal in Rome, first publishes the letter of Carli, 17.
Saguenay, Roberval in 1543 at, 41.
San Antonio, one of Magellan's ships, with Gomez, 118.
San Antonio, river on Ribero's map, 106.
Santa Cruz, Alonzo de, map of, in the Munich atlas, 42.
Santa Cruz, or Brazil, threatened expedition of Verrazzano, to, 139.
St. Domingo, Indians taken to, from South Carolina, 78 ; expeditions of Ayllon and Matienzo from, 123.
Santa Elena or Helena, South Carolina, Ayllon dies and his expedition ends there, 123.
Santiago, on the Ribero map, 43 ; on the Verrazzano map, 93.
St. Johns, Newfoundland, fishing vessels there in 1527, 63.
S. Juan, C. de, on the Ribero map, Cape Hatteras, 130.
St. Lawrence, the river, 37, 40.
Santa Maria, bay of, the Chesapeake, visited by Menendez Marquez, 50, 133.
Santa Maria, one of the Azores, treasure sent by Cortes, remains at, 142.
St. Roman, C. de, southerly limit of the Verrazzano voyage, 130.
St. Vincent, Cape, treasure captured off, 143.

Santee, the river Jordan, Indians taken from, 78 ; northerly limit of the expeditions of Ayllon, 123-4.
Saracens, complexion of the American Indians likened by Ramusio to the, 82.
Sarçales, on Ribero's map, at or near Cape Canso, 131.
Seville, charts showing the exploration of Gomez prepared at, 122, 126.
Silveira, Portuguese ambassador to France, 139; his letter to King João III, 141, 162.
Simancas, documents from the archives at, 148, 167, 168.
Smith, Buckingham, his inquiry into the authenticity of the Verrazzano discovery, 3; globe of Ulpius found by him, 113 ; documents obtained by him from the archives of Spain and Portugal, *prefatory note* and *Appendix*.
Smith, Capt. John, description of the complexion of the Indians of the Chesapeake, 78-9.
South Carolina discovered in the expedition of Ayllon and Matienzo, 119.
Spaniards discover Norumbega, 39 ; and Florida, 93.
Strozzi library in Florence, depository of the Carli manuscript, 11, 15 ; when founded, 11.
Sumatra, voyage to, 85.
Sylvanus, Bernardus, map in his edition of the Ptolemy of 1511, 60.

T.

Terra Nova, fisheries carried on there by the Portuguese in 1506, 61 ; Indians taken thence to France in 1508, 62-3 ; discovered by the Bretons and Normands and the Portuguese, 86-7.
Thomassey, M., first to call attention to the Verrazano map in 1853, 92 ; describes the Ribero map sent to the pope, 125.
Thevet, Andrè, his account of the Verrazzano voyage, 30.
Tiraboschi, mentions the Carli version of the letter, 13, 15 ; and the letter of Caro, 108.
Tobacco pipe, its use among the Indians of the North American continent, 74.
Toledo, Indians taken there by Gomez, 121.
Traffalgar, C. now Cape Fear, on the map of Ribera, the landfall of the Verrazzano voyage near, 130.

U.

Ulpius, Euphrosynus, globe of, 99 ; the only evidence of the early existence of the Verrazano map, 101, 113 ; from, 115.

V.

Val di Greve, Verrazzano a town in the, whence the family name, 134.
Varesam, Jehan de, agreement with Chabot, 35, 158, 160.

INDEX. 197

Varezano João, mentioned by the Portuguese chronicler, Andrade, 139; and by the ambassador, Silveira, 141, 163.

Verassen, Jean, mentioned in the manuscripts of Dieppe, 112.

Verrazano, Hieronimo de, map of, 84; map described, 91–115.

Verrazzana, land of, 94; sea of, 132.

Verrazzani, the brothers, 113, 115.

Verrazzano, family of, 13, 116, 134.

Verrazzano, Bernardo da, two ancestors of the name, 134.

Verrazzano, Giovanni da, the discovery attributed to him, 1; letter in his name addressed to the king of France, 3; letter not genuine, 10; two versions of the letter, 10; one first printed by Ramusio, in 1556, 10; the other appended to a letter of Fernando Carli, first printed in 1841, 11–13; the latter the original form, 13–16; the letter not authentic, 25; no voyage made by him for the king of France known in the history of France or acknowledged by her kings, 25–44; the letter intrinsically false, 45–83; stated by Hakluyt to have made three voyages to America and visited Henry VIII, of England, 109; his career, 134–148; Ramusio's account of his death, 134–5; was a corsair known by the name of Juan Florin, 136; his first capture, 138; threatens an expedition against Brazil, 139–141; captures the treasure sent from Mexico by Cortes, 143; takes a Portuguese Indiaman in the summer of 1524, 145; his probable visit to England, 146; enters into a venture with Chabot, 146; depredates upon the commerce of Spain and is himself captured, 147; summarily executed by order of Charles V, in November 1427, 148; not answerable for the fraud, 151.

Verrazzano, Piero Andrea da, father of Giovanni, 134.

Vespucci, Amerigo, 7, 52.

Vespucci, Juan, 120.

Victoria, one of Magellan's ships returns with the news of his death, 119.

W.

Wampum, used for money and personal ornament by the Indians of New England, 72–3.

Waymouth, Captain, Rosier's account of smoking the tobacco pipe by the Indians seen on his voyage, 74.

Williams, Roger, on the use of wampum by the Narraganset Indians, 73–4; on their complexion, 79.

Wolsey, Cardinal, proposition to Sebastian Cabot, in 1519, to go in search of a northwest passage, 113.

Wood, William, description of the wampum of the Narrangansets, 73.

X.

Xaragua, Bechechio Cacique of, 71.

Y.

Yucatan and Yucatanet on the Verrazano map, 95 *note*.

Z.

Z, the letter used differently in the name of the author of the map, and that of the navigator, 91 *map*, 94 *note*, 16 *note*, 134, 186.

PRESS OF J. MUNSELL.
ALBANY, N. Y.

We have received from Mr. Henry Harrisse of Paris copies, taken from the archives of the Parliament of Rouen, of two powers of attorney made by Verrazzano. They do not relate to his reputed voyage of discovery, but apparently refer to the projected voyage to the Indies for spices, and serve to establish the authenticity of the agreement with Chabot in regard to the latter voyage. They are important in so far as they fix the year 1526 as that in which the contract was made, corroborating the opinion which we expressed in that particular,[1] and conforming to the documents from the archives in Simancas in regard to the capture and execution of Verrazzano by the Spaniards. They also prove that Verrazzano had a brother Hieronimo, a relationship conceded[2] to the author of the map, in the Borgian collection,[3] bearing his name, though not ascertained, but regarded as of no practical importance, inasmuch as the mere consanguinity of these parties could not verify the representations on the map, even if they were made by Hieronimo, of which as yet there is no positive proof. Indeed on the contrary we are assured from Rome, on high authority, that this map appears to belong to a period subsequent to 1550, and is regarded by its custodians as only a copy at the best.

This note with the two papers from Rouen appended are intended as a supplement to the Memoir on the "Voyage of Verrazzano." H. C. M.

Brooklyn, April, 20, 1876.

---

[1] Page 35.
[2] Page 91.
[3] The Propaganda College in which this collection is found, is not in the Vatican, as inadvertently stated, but in the Via Due Macelli on the opposite side of the river.

Documents from the Archives of the Parliament of Rouen.

"*Du vendredi onze mai* 1526.

Noble homme Jehan de Varasenne, capitaine des navires esquippez pour aller au voyage des Indes, lequel fist, nomma, ordonna, constitua et estably son procureur general et certains messagiers especiaulx cest asscavoir Jerosme de Varasenne son frere et heritier et Zanobis de Rousselay en plaidoirie et par especial de recevoir tout ce qui au dit constituant est, sera peult et pourra estre deu par quelque personne et pour quelque cause ou causes que ce soit ou puisse estre tant à raison du dit voyage des Indes que autrement, du dit deu ensemble de ses descords et procez traicter, composer et appoincter par tels prix moiens et conditions que les dits Jerosme et de Rousselay pourront et de receu[r] et bailler quictance et descharge telle que mestier sera et generalement promettre, tenir et obliger biens et heriritages—presents m[el] Gales et Nicolas Doublet.

Janus Verrazanus."

Sur le même feuillet :

"*Du samedi douzieme jour de mai* 1526.

Noble homme Messire Jehan de Varasenne, capitaine des navires esquippez pour aller au voiage des Indes, confessa avoir commis, constitué et estably Adam Godeffroy, bourgeois de Rouen auqel il a donné et donne par ces presentes pouvoir et puissance de faire pour le dit de Verrassane[1] en ung des dits navires nommé la Barque de Fescamp, du port de quatre vingt et dix tonneualx ou environ dont est maistre, aprez Dieu, Pierre Cauuay pour ouicelluy navire faire traffiquer et negossier par le dit Varrassenne en toutes choses pour le dit voiage des Indes ainsi que par le dit de Varrassene sera baillé par articles et memoires soubz son seing audit Godeffroy. Et pour ce faire le dit

---

[1] Les mots " en sa charge de capitaine es dits navires," sont ici rayés dans l'original, et l'on ajouté en marge ceux-ci : " et pour le dit Godeffroy."

de Varrasene a promis payer au dit Godeffroy pour sa peine et vaccation de farie et accomplir les dits articles et memoires à son pouvoir en faisant le dit voiage de la dite barque la somme de cinq cents livres tournois et icelle somme payer au retour du dit voiage a quoi faire le dit de Varassene a obligé et oblige tous ses biens meubles et heritages et iceulx prendre par execution incontinent le dit retour.— Et aussi le dit Godefroy s'est submis faire le dit voyage et deuement et loyaument servir le dit de Varassenne et accomplir à son pouvoir les dits articles et memoires qui ainsi lui seront baillez par le dit de Varrassenne.— Et est ce sans préjudice des biens, deniers et marchandises que le dit Godeffroy aura et pourra mettre es dits navires pour faire le dit voiage, lesquels lui et les siens auront avec eux emportez pour le profit d'iceulx oultre la dite somme de cinq cents livres tournois pour le dit voyage et a ce tenir obligent par l'un et l'autre chacun en son regard leurs biens et heritages.—Presents Jehan Desvaulx et Robert Boutou."

(Translation.)

Friday the Eleventh of May, 1526.

Jehan de Varasenne, nobleman, captain of the ships equipped to go on the voyage to the Indies, has made, named, ordained, constituted and instituted his attorney, and certain special commissioners, that is to say, Jerosme de Varasenne his brother and heir and Zanobis de Rousselay, to sue and especially to receive all which to the said principal is, shall be, may and may become due by any person and for any cause or causes whatsoever as regards what is thus due as well by reason of the said voyage to the Indies as otherwise; and also his disagreements and law suits to treat compound and settle by such prices, means and conditions as the said Jerosme and de Rousselay shall be able to do, and to receive and receipt for and discharge according as the case may be, and generally to pledge, hold and bind chattels and lands.

Present m^{el} Gales and Nicolas Doublet.

JANUS VERRAZANUS.

On the same leaf:

Saturday the Twelfth day of May, 1526.

Messire Jehan de Varasenne, nobleman, captain of the ships equipped to go on the voyage to the Indies acknowledged that he had appointed, constituted and instituted Adam Godeffroy citizen of Rouen, to whom he has given and gives by these presents power and authority to act for the said de Varrasenne[1] in one of the said ships named the barque of Fescamp of the burthen of ninety tons or thereabouts, of which the master is, after God, Pierre Cauvay, the which ship to employ in trading and traffic for the said Varrasenne in all things for the said voyage of the Indies as by the said de Varrassenne shall be directed by articles and memoranda under his sign manual to the said Godeffroy. And for doing this the said de Varrasenne has promised to pay to the said Godeffroy for his trouble and time and attention in doing and fulfilling the said articles and memoranda according to his ability in making the said voyage of the said barque, the sum of five hundred pounds Tours currency, and this sum to pay on the return from the said voyage, to do which the said de Varassene has bound and binds all his chattels and lands, and to take them by execution immediately on the said return. And in like manner the said Godeffroy has undertaken to make the said voyage and duly and loyally to serve the said de Varasenne, and to carry out according to his power the said articles and memoranda which thus shall be given by the said de Varrassenne.

And it is without prejudice of the goods, funds and merchandise which the said Godeffroy shall have and might place on the said ships to make the said voyage, which he and his shall have carried away with them, for their profit, besides the said sum of five hundred pounds Tours currency for the said voyage. And to keep this, each for himself, both parties bind themselves, their chattels and lands.

Present Jehan Desvaulx and Robert Bouton.

---

[1] The words "in his quality of captain of the said ships" are here erased in the original, and they have added in the margin these; "and for the said Godeffroy."

Printed in Dunstable, United Kingdom